WITHDRAWN

GREEN, C.   F.

Coronation Street: The way to Victory.

PERTH AND KINROSS COUNCIL
LEISURE & CULTURAL SERVICES
LIBRARIES & ARCHIVES DIVISION

This book is due for return on or before the last date indicated on label. Renewals may be obtained on application.

CORONATION ST: THE WAY TO VICTORY

Continuing the enthralling saga of the Street at War

1943: As the war grinds on, life is hard on Coronation Street. The German bombing continues, the Yanks have been posted overseas and Elsie Tanner sets out on a potentially disastrous search for excitement... Down the street Ida Barlow waits anxiously for news of her husband Frank and Annie Walker gets a new glint in her eye when discreetly pursued by the local headmaster. Local girl Hilda Crabtree finds love in the blackout when she trips over a drunk Stan Ogden. Full of romance, scandal and humour, this book is sure to delight the programme's many fans.

CORONATION ST:
THE WAY TO VICTORY

Coronation St: The Way To Victory

by

Christine Green

Magna Large Print Books
Long Preston, North Yorkshire,
BD23 4ND, England.

British Library Cataloguing in Publication Data.

Green, Christine
    Coronation St: The way to victory.

    A catalogue record of this book is
    available from the British Library

    ISBN   0-7505-1791-3

First published in Great Britain in 2000
by Granada Media, an imprint of André Deutsch Limited

Text Copyright © Granada Media Group Limited 2000

Cover illustration by arrangement with
Granada Media Group Limited.

Published in Large Print 2002 by arrangement with
Granada Media Group Limited

Magna Large Print is an imprint of Library Magna Books Ltd.

Printed and bound in Great Britain by
T.J. (International) Ltd., Cornwall, PL28 8RW

CHAPTER ONE

Summer 1943: Mussolini Overthrown

'Sodom and Gomorrah,' announced Ena, with feet splayed and eyes flashing as she stared at the poster stuck on *her* noticeboard outside the Glad Tidings Mission Hall. She had a broom in one hand so she stuck that under her arm and tore down the offending item. 'Sodom and Gomorrah,' she repeated.

A voice from behind startled her. 'What's to do, Mrs Sharples?'

She turned swiftly. 'Oh, it's you, Albert Tatlock. You wouldn't think there was a war on in Weatherfield, would you?' She didn't give him time to answer but thrust the offending poster in front of his nose so that he had to take a step back to see it properly. 'It's a disgrace, that's what it is, a bloomin' disgrace.'

Although his eyesight was poor and his glasses were thick he could easily see the can-can dancer's red bloomers. 'Oh, aye.'

'Is that all you can say – "oh, aye"? Don't

you think it's a disgrace? All this lot in Coronation Street think about is dancing and someone from round 'ere has dared to stick it on *my* noticeboard.'

Albert shrugged. 'My dancin' days is over, Mrs Sharples. I'm on me way to join a queue.'

'What for?' she asked, suddenly interested.

'Who knows? But I did read in the paper as 'ow someone's seen a banana.'

Mrs Sharples propped her broom by the noticeboard, rolled up the poster, which advertised a dance next Saturday night at the church hall, and stuffed it under her arm. 'I'll find out who stuck this 'ere if it's the last thing I do. I'm the caretaker 'ere, after all. We can all manage without bananas but pictures showin' – showin' everything is a different matter.'

'Aye,' repeated Albert. 'You comin' to join the queue?'

To Ena, finding the culprit came before queuing – there was always a queue to join. 'I'm seeing Elsie Tanner first. She's behind this. People round 'ere are getting lax. Only last week there was a dance and when the siren went off only four people left and came to my shelter.'

'Right then, I'm off,' said Albert. 'Mrs

Foyle might have summat tasty on sale.'

Ena watched for a moment as Albert walked off to join the queue at the Corner Shop, then she picked up her broom, put it back in the cupboard, removed her apron and stomped down the street. First stop, No. 11 – young Elsie Tanner's.

At Elsie's Ena knocked hard enough to disturb half the Street. A few curtains twitched but the residents were well used to the regular stand-up barneys between Ena and Elsie. It was nine o'clock in the morning and the sun was shining, but Elsie's curtains were still closed. Ena gave up knocking and yelled through the letterbox, 'Elsie Tanner! I know you're in there! I want a word with you.'

There was still no answer. 'Lazy madam,' muttered Ena. By now she'd begun to think again about the queue. She had her ration books tucked in her apron pocket and nothing much in her larder. And she needed soap. Elsie Tanner would have to wait. 'I'll be back,' she shouted. Then she laid the poster over her shoulder as if it were a rifle and marched off to join the queue.

Elsie Tanner lay in bed smoking a Woodbine. She'd no idea why Ena Sharples was on the warpath and she didn't care. Like the bombers, Ena always came back. All Elsie thought about in quiet moments was Steve Tanner, her American GI. One letter – that was all she'd had. He was on the move, he'd said, he'd write again when he knew where he'd be based. Twice a day the postman delivered mail but there was nothing from the USA. She pushed to the back of her mind the idea that he might have found someone else. After all *she* had scarcely seen a man since Steve had left in May.

She puffed on her fag and watched the smoke-rings. The room was dark because of the blackout curtains but at least the kids weren't screaming yet. She'd spent most of the night in the basement shelter of the Glad Tidings Mission Hall and her Dennis was teething – he'd screamed the place down. Poor little bugger had nappy rash too. Was it the kids Ena had come about? She was always saying they were pasty-faced and would get rickets if Elsie wasn't careful. Voice of doom, Ena could be, but she had done Elsie some favours in the past – one of which had been tricking the Military Police so that she could say goodbye to Steve. She could still remember the feel of his lips, her head snuggling into his shoulder that last

12

time. He'd stroked her hair and said he loved her. What a difference there was between him and her old man Arnold! He'd rip her knickers off without a by-your-leave – just a grunt and 'I love your bum'.

The trouble with Arnold was that she'd married him. At sixteen. She'd had to – her Linda was on the way. She was three now, and bright as a button. Her Linda and Arnold's Navy pay were the only things to recommend him. Arnold had got her pregnant on his last leave. At least she was *sure* it was him. Some women weren't too certain who had fathered their children. In wartime no one asked too many questions about the timing of leave. At least, not to your face. Behind backs there was always gossip. Even about those women who daren't look at a man for fear of getting pregnant.

The Americans, in Elsie's opinion, had been well prepared for wartime Britain. They had lovely muscled bodies, nylons, cigarettes, chocolates and johnnies. If it weren't for some self-control and the johnnies many a GI would have left behind more than fags and nylons.

'Mam … Mam,' whined Linda, as she walked into Elsie's bedroom with a snotty nose and a bare bum. 'I've wet the bed, Mam.'

'You always do, pet,' Elsie said, as she pulled back the bedcovers and the little girl with her cold bum got in beside her.

'I love your bed, Mam.'

Elsie smiled and lifted her arm up so that Linda could snuggle down. 'Go back to sleep, love.'

One more Woodbine later Dennis began bawling and a Saturday of washing sheets and nappies stretched before her.

Ena joined the 'blind' queue. Folk called it that because the queues were so long you couldn't see what was being sold. She usually barged to the top and waylaid someone who'd just been served, then she'd announce the purchase to the rest. Some women left the queue immediately, perhaps a bit put out that they didn't need that particular item, but most stayed because anything you bought that you didn't want you could always swap or sell on. Today she didn't do that because Minnie Caldwell was at the back end.

'Hello, Ena,' she said. 'It's a nice day. What's for sale?'

'Never mind the weather, Minnie Caldwell. And how would I know? I've just joined the queue. It'll give me time to simmer down.'

'What's wrong, Ena? Who's upset you?'

'This,' Ena took the poster from her shoulder, unrolled it and held it up. A few in the queue turned round to look. 'Mind your own business,' said Ena loudly, and they turned back.

Minnie smiled. 'Ooh, Ena, it's lovely and bright,' she said.

'Lovely and bright, Minnie Caldwell? Is that all you can say? My Mission Hall is lovely and bright. This is…' she searched for the word '…rude.'

'If you say so, Ena. But I like paintings.'

'It isn't a bloomin' paintin', it's an advertisement. Sometimes, Minnie, you can be as slow as our Vera.'

'She's not slow, Ena. Not now … not now she's grown-up.'

'In my eyes, Minnie Caldwell, she'll never be grown-up.'

'That's as maybe, Ena, but–'

'Don't go off the subject, Minnie,' said Ena. 'I reckon Elsie Tanner's responsible for this. She'll be over that namesake of hers, Steve Tanner, by now and want to be out gallivantin'. And if she asks you to keep an eye on 'er kids, say no. She's always palmin' off those kids on all and sundry. And I'm sure she only feeds them on chips and bread and marge.'

'What's that got to do with the poster, Ena? I didn't know Elsie could paint.'

Minnie had a point and Ena paused, but only for a second. 'I'm sure she's only good at one thing and you know what *that* is. But she'll be behind it and when I've finished standin' 'ere gettin' varicose veins I'll be along to Number eleven to 'ave it out with 'er.'

'Yes, Ena,' said Minnie, with a little smile.

It was nearly eleven when Ena returned to do battle at No. 11. This time Elsie was up and dressed, wearing bright red lipstick, her cheeks rouged with the same colour. For a moment Ena forgot her mission. 'If you took as much trouble over your own kids as you do paintin' your face, Elsie Tanner, they'd be a lot healthier.'

'Is that it, Mrs Sharples? I'm young and I want to look nice. That's not a bloody crime, is it?'

'No, but this is,' said Ena, producing the poster from behind her back.

'Well, you'd better come in, Mrs Sharples,

before you make an exhibition of yourself on my doorstep.'

Sometimes, but not often, twenty-year-old Elsie got the better of Ena Sharples, and this was one of them. Not for the first time Ena realized that she and Elsie had something in common. She couldn't condone Elsie's loose morals but the girl had spirit and, grudgingly, she admired that. 'Right, then, I'll come in,' said Ena, trying to sound as if it had been her idea.

Dennis lay on his back, kicking his legs in the middle of the back room on an old blanket, wearing only a grey-looking vest. Linda was playing with some cards and from the scullery came the smell of boiling nappies. Suddenly Ena's irritation began to disappear. Elsie wasn't a good housewife but she tried – and, after all, being married at sixteen and losing her mam and dad in an air-raid must have been terrible for her.

'Take a seat,' said Elsie. 'Get it off your chest, Mrs Sharples.'

Ena's hackles rose at Elsie's cocky tone. 'It's this,' she said, unfurling the evidence.

'That's nowt to do with me,' said Elsie, taking more notice of the place and date than of the can-can dancer. 'Never seen it before.'

'Aye, well, you would say that.'

Elsie fixed Ena with a hard stare. 'I may be a lot of things in your opinion, Mrs Sharples, but I'm not a liar.' Before Ena could answer Elsie carried on. 'And I don't think there's anything wrong with that poster. We all have legs and we all wear panties – some bigger than others. Even the Queen.'

Ena was outraged. 'How dare you! The Queen wouldn't flaunt herself.'

'I'm not sayin' she would. I'm just sayin' she's got legs and wears bloomers, and I don't know nothin' about your poster.'

'It seems I've come to the wrong place,' said Ena stiffly.

'You certainly have. You're only peeved because the church is puttin' on the do, not your miserable old Mission Hall.'

At that moment Dennis, beginning to bawl, rolled over on to his front. Ena's sharp eyes couldn't fail to see the sight of his blistered bum. She had a soft spot for babies, had delivered dozens as the unofficial local midwife – she had even brought Elsie's kids into the world. Which was why nothing would stop her if she had something to say about the welfare of 'her' babies.

'Poor little mite,' she said. 'You should be ashamed of yourself, letting him get in this state.'

'He's teethin', and I forgot to take a clean nappy with me in the raid last night.'

Ena looked across at Elsie as she lit a cigarette. It wasn't smoke bringing those tears to her eyes. She softened her tone. 'You're doing right,' she said. 'Let the air get to 'is bum and make up a paste with some starch and water and put that on. And in future remember I always 'ave a few spare nappies. Lovely and soft they are too.' Ena cooed at the baby for a while, and although she sniffed at the sight of Linda with the playing cards, she played Snap with her while Elsie made a brew.

'What are you feedin' these kids on, Elsie?'

'They don't go 'ungry.'

'Are you tekkin' them to the clinic?'

'I get what's goin' for them.'

'Your Dennis looks as if he never sees the sun.'

Elsie stood up and folded her arms. 'Thanks for the advice, Mrs Sharples. Perhaps you'd ask the Almighty for an extra sun ration for my kids – and while you're at it, ask Him to put a stop to the war so that us women can have a bit of a break.'

19

'It's a pity your Arnold isn't–'

'It's a pity my Arnold was ever born, Mrs Sharples.'

They stared at each other for a moment. But Mrs Sharples had to have the last word. At the door she said, 'At least you 'ave a good chance of seein' 'im again. More than can be said for that fancy piece Steve Tanner.'

Before Elsie could respond, Ena had slammed the front door shut.

'Mam – Mam!' called Linda.

'Oh, shut up,' said Elsie, 'or I'll put you through the mangle with the nappies.'

'Mam, I'm 'ungry,' whined Linda, pulling at Elsie's skirt.

Elsie patted her head. 'We won't let that silly old moo get us down, will we? I'll do you some bread and marge with a bit o' Spam.'

CHAPTER TWO

Autumn 1943: Allied Invasion of Italy Begins

The Rovers smelt of damp clothes and rough tobacco. Saturday night was the busiest of the week. Outside it was raining pailfuls and Annie Walker admonished those who came through her portals with wet feet. 'Please be kind enough to wipe your feet, ladies and gentlemen.' Then she added, for good measure, 'Remember where you are.'

'You're right, Mrs Walker,' said one of the ARP wardens on his rounds. 'This *is* hallowed ground, but just make sure you observe the blackout.'

Annie, hand on pump as she drew a half-pint of mild for Albert Tatlock, said archly, 'I always do. I'm very fussy about observing the regulations.'

'Worse than a sergeant major,' someone muttered, but Annie didn't see who had said it so she carried on serving Albert, who had come in for a game of dominoes and a bit of warmth.

In the Snug Ena had taken off her damp coat but she still felt cold. 'You'd think Annie Walker could keep the place warmer than this,' she said loudly to Martha Longhurst, who sat staring into her glass of milk stout. 'What's up wi' you?' asked Ena.

'Nothin' a hot summer's day by the sea wouldn't put right.'

'Well,' said Ena, 'when the war's over they'll tek all that barbed wire down and we'll go to Blackpool for the day.'

'Will we really, Ena?' said Minnie Caldwell, lifting her glass. 'That would be lovely.'

'I've just said we would. There's nowt to do now but get on with it.'

'I 'ate the winter,' said Martha.

'You 'ate all the seasons of the year, Martha Longhurst. It's no good you sittin' there with a face like a busted cabbage. Think yoursel' lucky.'

'Lucky? I've got nowt to feel lucky about.'

'You've only got yoursel' to worry about. Your Percy's soft as soap and your Lily loves nothin' better than a bit o' housework. You can do what you like when you like. And you've got a little job charring. No responsibilities. Thank the Almighty for that. Some poor women round 'ere are really strugglin'.'

'You're right,' Ena,' said Minnie. 'There's lots worse off.'

Ena gave her a scathing look. 'You was one of them I was thinkin' of.'

Minnie thought about that for a moment. 'What do you mean, Ena?'

'I mean,' said Ena, 'that mother of yours runs you ragged.'

'She's right poorly, she can't 'elp that.'

Ena sniffed. 'Lazy, more like. Just lays abed with you scurryin' around like a frightened rabbit.'

'I like looking after my mam,' said Minnie quietly. 'And I've got my Mabel.'

'I reckon you go without food to feed that cat of yours.'

'No I don't, Ena. I don't get any thinner, do I?'

Ena cast a glance over Minnie's rounded little body. 'Can't expect to at our age. A woman gets fat in her forties.'

'Martha doesn't.'

Ena shrugged. 'I reckon Martha Longhurst lives on fresh air and misery.'

'What yer blatherin' about?' said Martha.

'Your brain's gettin' addled,' said Ena. 'There's none so deaf as those that can 'ear.'

Martha, with her most animated expression since the outbreak of war, pointed a finger at the window. 'Nothin' wrong with my brain. I was lookin' at that blackout curtain.'

Ena gave the floor-length curtains a glance. They *were* moving. 'We'll see about this,' she said, and marched over to the window.

'Ena always has to be first,' commented Minnie. 'I do admire her.'

'Don't be so soft,' said Martha. 'It'll be nowt but a cat or summat.'

Startled, Minnie stood up. 'It could be my Mabel – she might 'ave followed me in.'

Martha grabbed Minnie's arm to pull her back down. 'Let Ena deal with it.'

By now Ena was the centre of attention. 'Come out,' she boomed, 'and show your-sel'.' The curtain twitched but Ena could wait no longer. Wary of breaking the blackout, she kicked at the lump.

'Ow!' Out came a fair-haired little boy.

'Billy Walker, what *are* you doin'?'

In his hand he held a nearly empty half-pint mug. Beer foam was round his mouth and some had dribbled down his pyjamas.

Annie Walker nearly fainted on the spot. She had never felt so mortified in her whole life. When she *did* find her voice she sounded as if someone had strangled her.

'Billy, get to your room – at once!' He scampered out, grinning, with Annie behind him.

'That took that smell-under-her-nose look off her face,' said Ena, as she sat down. 'I'll be 'avin' words with 'er about young Billy.'

'The trouble with you, Ena,' murmured Minnie, 'is that you and Annie Walker both think you're better than anyone else.'

Ena's withering look would have rotted compost but Minnie didn't seem to notice. Both Ena and Annie were proud. It *was* a sin, Ena knew, and the good Lord knew it, but she'd been made that way and she couldn't change. All she could do was pray. 'That's as maybe,' she said, 'but I don't put on airs and graces.'

'That's true enough,' said Minnie. 'You're always Ena.'

When Annie Walker finally emerged she put on a brave smile, saying, 'Just a minor misdemeanour.'

Albert Tatlock, waiting for a third half, said, 'That's what Chamberlain thought before 'Itler invaded Poland.'

'Mr Tatlock, I'm surprised at you. My Billy is good as gold. It's because he's going to Bessie Street School now. All sorts of ideas they've given him. He only started in

September and already he's the best reader in the class.'

'Oh, aye,' said Albert, hand outstretched for his beer.

Ena came up behind him and said, 'I expect 'Itler was a good reader, Albert Tatlock. What do you think?'

He clutched his ale and took a swig. 'Aye, 'spect 'e was.' He moved away sharpish, knowing a skirmish was ahead.

Ena leaned over the bar and fixed Annie with an icy stare. 'A word of well-meant Christian advice, Mrs Walker.'

Annie squared up to her full height of five foot three. 'Yes, Mrs Sharples. I thought you might want to have your say.'

'There's no need to take that tone wi' me, Mrs Walker. I'm just bein' friendly. With your Jack away, you want to do what's best, don't you?'

'Of course. Boys will be boys.'

'Aye, but you expect more of your Billy don't you?'

Annie Walker's shoulders relaxed a little. 'Yes, of course I do. I want him to be different.'

'I suppose by that you mean – not like the lads round 'ere.'

Annie nodded.

'Well, in that case you can't run an ale-house and look after young 'uns, 'specially your Billy.'

'What are you suggesting, Mrs Sharples?'

'You need a body to 'elp you. Make sure 'e stays in bed of an evening. Play wi' 'im for a bit and keep 'im out of mischief.'

'What sort of helpful body?'

'Go down the school and find a school leaver to live in. Some young lass would be grateful for a job wi' bed and board.'

Annie let the idea sink in. 'I don't know if I could afford a ... nanny.'

'You can afford a few shillings a week, Mrs Walker. A woman like you 'as a bit stashed away for a rainy day. The lass could stay till your Jack comes home for good.'

'A nanny,' murmured Annie. It was music to her ears. Why hadn't she thought of it before?

'Don't make the poor lass a skivvy within a week,' warned Ena, wagging her finger. 'You overwork her and she'll be tailin' it down the munitions factory as fast as some 'ere sup their ale.'

'I'll think about it, Mrs Sharples. Thank you for your advice.'

'Don't just think about – do summat!'

Ena walked back to her seat, smiling.

27

'There you are, Martha, I win,' Minnie declared.

'What's bin goin' on?' asked Ena, looking from one woman to the other.

'I had a little bet on and I've won,' giggled Minnie.

'What have I told you about the evils of gamblin'? You should be ashamed.'

'Well, I'm not this time, Ena. Martha's gettin' the milk stouts, aren't you, Martha?'

Martha stood up, looking grim, and walked to the bar.

'Come on, Minnie,' said Ena, the thought of a free drink easing her disapproval. 'What the 'eck were you bettin' on?'

Minnie's round, pretty face smiled. 'I bet you'd 'ave the last word with Annie Walker. Well done, Ena.'

They'd only just started their drinks when the siren sounded. Ena thrust her ARP helmet on immediately. 'Right,' she said. 'Follow me.'

No one moved. 'Come on, you lot,' she called out, 'war's not over yet.'

Still no one moved. Eventually Minnie said timidly, 'We're going into Mrs Walker's cellar for this one. She's got some lovely Glenn Miller records.'

Ena bristled with annoyance, reminding

28

Minnie of a cat with its fur on end. 'Next you'll be tellin' me you lot are tired of the "The Old Rugged Cross" and "Abide With Me".'

'The war's been on a long time, Ena,' said Minnie. 'We need a change.'

As Ena walked off, only Albert Tatlock followed her. He, too, was an ARP warden so he didn't have a choice. Ena was aware that Annie Walker's eyes were on her back and that she was feeling she'd won some sort of victory. So she turned and stared the landlady in the eye. 'Never forget,' she said in a loud voice, 'the lads round 'ere may be rough round the edges but they all went to Bessie Street School and they're 'eroes – 'eroes every one of them.'

Churchill could have taken lessons from me, thought Ena, as she strode off into the dark with the sirens still blaring. Annie Walker might have thought she'd bested Ena on this one but defeat wasn't a word she knew. By 'eck it wasn't.

The raid was a short one, over by midnight, and Annie Walker was glad to have her cellar empty. It had been a long day and although the cellarman had done the heavy lifting she had been constantly on her feet and there were always Billy and Joan to keep an eye on. Even getting a char was difficult these days. The wages in the munitions factories were good and single women had joined the services in huge numbers. If she'd been single Annie would have wanted to entertain the troops. Her voice was as good as Gracie Fields's, and anything in that line would have been better than being stuck at the Rovers with only rough types to talk to. The trouble was, none of them wanted to better themselves. Even her Jack didn't have much ambition. To him, running the Rovers was the pinnacle of success. He'd told her he wanted a quiet life after the war, get to know young Billy and baby Joan, who was just beginning to toddle about and in her fourteen months had only seen her father twice. Annie wanted more. Other women, the young ones anyway, had been out to dances and enjoyed themselves – married or not. She had been stuck wiping up slops and trying to keep an air of decorum in the bar. From morning to night she was like a mole, rarely seeing daylight. She tried to make the best of herself, but why bother? Folks in Coronation Street thought she was a joke just because she had standards.

As she lay in bed that night the thought of

having a nanny cheered her. Billy wouldn't get into mischief again and everyone round here would see that *her* children were far superior to the likes of the Tanners – all snotty-nosed and ill-bred.

Tomorrow, she thought, I'll be down that Bessie Street School to find a nice refined girl to look after the children. The war will soon be over. Jack will be back and then everything will be better. Perhaps the amateur dramatic society will start up again. Even better was the thought that they could move to the country, live among more genteel people. For now, though, a nanny would have to do. Royalty had nannies, didn't they? And look how well *they* turned out.

At No. 1 Albert Tatlock banked up the fire with more wood. His wife Bessie had made a brew, and although it was the middle of the night they didn't want to go to bed. The bedroom was like an icebox, and many a night they sat at either side of the fire talking, mostly about Beattie, their daughter, who had been evacuated to the countryside at the start of the war aged five. Bessie held her cup with both hands to get a bit of warmth into them. 'The war might be over soon, Albert,' she said. 'Did we do the right thing in lettin' 'er go away?'

'We didn't 'ave much choice, did we? An' she's 'avin a good life there. That woman who took her in 'as treated 'er like her own.'

Bessie nodded and stared into the fire. 'Too much so for my likin'. All that trouble we 'ad when she wanted to adopt 'er.'

'Aye, but she didn't, so it's no good frettin' about it now, is it, hen?'

He patted her knee, and Bessie's eyes filled with tears. 'Last time I saw her she seemed to 'ardly know me. And toys and lovely clothes – I didn't know there were such things.'

'She'll settle down when she comes back to us,' said Albert, giving the fire a good poke.

Bessie sighed. 'She talks so posh now they'll tease the life out of 'er at school.'

'She'll soon talk as rough as the others.'

'Yes, Albert, but will she like it?'

'She'll have to lump it, won't she?'

Bessie fell quiet then, for Albert's mouth had set like concrete. Best humour him, she thought.

'At least Ida Barlow, and young Kenneth and David need me.'

'Aye,' said Albert. 'With Frank away, I

don't know 'ow she would have managed wi'out you.'

'Is that true? 'Cos I don't know 'ow I'd 'ave managed without them.'

'There you are, then. All sorted. How about another brew, or 'as the kettle bust?'

Bessie smiled. Albert was back in a good humour, and as she busied herself in the kitchen brewing tea and spreading some pork dripping on toast she felt a lot brighter altogether. Her Albert loved his food, and she always managed to make something tasty. You had to count your blessings, she told herself. One was knowing her Beattie was safe and well fed. The other was her Albert. He was a rock in times of trouble. You're a lucky woman, she told herself. And the war was coming to an end, so the papers and the Pathé News said, so it must be true. After the war everything would be easier, she was sure of that.

CHAPTER THREE

Autumn 1943: Italy Declares War on Germany

Annie Walker powdered her nose lightly and applied lipstick carefully. She wanted to look smart and she still had a few good frocks from before the war. She'd shortened them to be fashionable, and now as she looked at herself in the mirror she felt satisfied. The added white collar above the powder pink frock made it look brand new. She slipped on her grey overcoat with its fox-fur edging, and felt grand enough to meet Bessie Street Senior's headmaster.

Martha Longhurst was keeping an eye on Joan and Billy was at school. Although the new cellarman, Ned Narkin, had a shifty look, he seemed to know what he was doing and would be on the pub premises until she got back. Her world was organized, and as Annie walked towards Bessie Street she felt cheerful, in spite of the drizzle and the drab houses. With so many men away the women had neither the time nor money to deal with decorating: the paint on most doors was peeling and the window-frames would barely last another winter.

Bessie Street School was an old Victorian building with iron railings and windows so high that the children couldn't see out of them. Inside it smelt of Izal and damp shoes, and it reminded Annie of a public lavatory. Her footsteps echoed on the shiny wooden floors, and as she made her way to the headmaster's office, she passed quiet classrooms where children sat dipping their pens into inkwells as they copied work from the blackboard. She remembered her own schooldays and how she had always striven not to make any blots and how if she did make the odd mistake she got very upset. So far she hadn't seen a soul, save for an elderly caretaker with a mop and bucket who pointed her silently in the right direction.

When she knocked on the office door a deep voice boomed. 'Come in,' and just for a moment she felt a little nervous.

When she entered the headmaster's sanctum she *still* felt that way. John Barnstable was a tall, handsome man in his early forties, with striking brown eyes and thick wavy hair. She'd always liked older men and his refined accent impressed her, so much so that her legs felt wobbly. 'I'm so grateful for a few minutes of your valuable time,' she said.

Smiling, he shook her hand. 'Do sit down, Mrs Walker,' he said. 'My secretary is away at the moment. The house next door to hers was bombed last night. Otherwise she would have been here to make you a cup of tea.'

Annie did not take her eyes off his face. 'I wondered, Mr Barnstable,' she began, 'if you had a suitable school leaver who would be interested in being a nanny to my two children. Someone refined and respectable, you understand. I'm a businesswoman, you see, and my husband is away so I want the best.'

'Of course you do, Mrs Walker. May I say that you look too young to have children. The responsibility has rested on you lightly.'

Annie felt herself blushing. His eyes were twinkling and she remembered how Jack had looked at her in the early days of their courtship.

'I do have one or two girls who would fit the bill,' he said, 'but of course, these days they have so many choices. Let me just check their record cards.' He walked to a cupboard, took out several brown envelopes and began reading through them. 'Do you

36

have any preferences?'

'Preferences?' she queried.

'Religious preferences.'

She shook her head. 'Not at all. As long as the girl is well-spoken, reliable, clean, tidy and good with children, I shall be happy.'

He smiled at her again. 'You seem to be a young woman who knows what she wants.'

'I do,' said Annie. 'My ambition is to live in the countryside away from all this.' She waved her hand towards the grimy window.

'Likewise,' said John Barnstable.

In that moment Annie sensed she had found a soul mate.

'Would you like to peruse these report cards,' he asked, 'while I find us a glass of sherry.'

There was nothing Annie would have liked better. By the time she had drunk her sherry she knew that he was single, enjoyed concerts and poetry, that he'd enlisted, but a problem with his Achilles tendon had precluded him from active service so he'd joined the Home Guard.

When she disclosed her address he said, 'You don't look tough enough to be running a public house on your own.'

Annie smiled. 'I'm tougher than I look.'

He would write, he said, when he'd made

37

arrangements for her to interview the girls she'd deemed suitable.

As she was leaving he shook her gloved hand and seemed to hold on to it for ages. 'Perhaps one evening,' he said tentatively, 'with your husband's permission, of course, we could attend a concert together.'

When she paused, he added. 'My mother could come too, which would be ... more proper.'

Annie didn't know whether to be glad or sorry about his mother. 'That would be most acceptable,' she said primly.

On the way back to the Rovers she smiled at the idea of getting Jack's permission. The post was so unreliable that she would have been to the concert before he received a letter. Anyway, she rarely went out, and if his mother was coming with them that made it respectable. Didn't it?

At the Rovers Martha Longhurst greeted her: 'I was wonderin' where you'd got to.'

Annie smiled. Today even the Martha Longhursts of Weatherfield couldn't dampen her spirits.

As Martha slipped on her overcoat, woollen mittens and black beret she noticed Annie Walker looking in the mirror above the fireplace smiling at her own reflection.

'Everythin' all right, Mrs Walker?'

'Everything is fine, Mrs Longhurst. Thank you for asking.'

Martha hurried along the street to the Mission of Glad Tidings. She'd never seen Annie Walker so cheerful before, but she knew Ena would know what to make of it.

At No. 3 Ida Barlow looked at the clock on the mantelpiece. It was time to collect her Kenneth from school. He'd started in September at Bessie Street Infants and although his teacher said he was doing well he often seemed tearful when he came home. David, who was only two, sat on the floor stacking empty cotton reels, every so often toddling towards her, arms out-stretched, for a cuddle. Ida had found David easier than Kenneth: he had a sunny, easy-going nature while Kenneth was always quiet and serious.

Ida walked to the school with David, and smiled at the few mothers who were waiting. Many of the five- and six-year-olds walked home alone – there was little traffic and always someone to look out for them.

When Kenneth came out of the school door she could see him looking for her anxiously. When he finally caught sight of her he ran towards her and grabbed her hand tightly. 'Did you have a nice day, pet?' she asked. He didn't answer, just lowered his head and watched his feet. He always avoided the cracks in the pavement, saying it was bad luck to step on them.

On the way home he hardly spoke. David was trotting along, chewing at one of his mittens. Ida smiled indulgently with a son on each side. Her little men.

'He's always doing that,' said Kenneth, pulling his brother's hand from his mouth.

David screeched.

'Now look what you've done,' said Ida. 'Leave our David alone!'

Once they were home she made fingers of toast with treacle but Kenneth refused to eat. David ate the lot, and before Ida had a chance to stop him had smeared sticky fingers on one of his brother's books.

'He shouldn't run round eating,' said Kenneth, snatching back his book and looking angry. 'It's not right.'

Ida sighed. Kenneth sometimes sounded like a little old man. Everything will be all right when Frank comes home, she told herself.

'Can I go out, Mam?' asked Kenneth a little later.

'You mean next door?'

He nodded.

'Well, don't be a nuisance and don't be long.'

The Hayes family lived at No. 5. Ada was a teacher at Bessie Street School, and Kenneth seemed happier with her, which made Ida wonder what she was doing wrong. He still wet the bed at night, which worried her, but Ada Hayes said most children did it because of all the disturbed nights they'd had. But it was all right for *her* to say that when she had no children of her own. It was getting the sheets dry in wet weather that was the problem. Ida stared across at the clothes-horse by the fire. It was always up, and David loved to drag the wet things on the floor.

It was Friday night. Bath night. Ida began to fill the kettle and a few saucepans. She prayed there wouldn't be a raid before they'd finished.

Elsie Tanner's Friday night treat was going to the pictures. The kids were in bed and she sat smoking and reading the local paper. There were several cinemas to choose from; the Ritz was showing *In Which We Serve,* but she didn't see the point of watching war films these days. On at the Bijou was *Gone With the Wind,* which was more her cup of tea. She'd seen it before but anything with Clark Gable in was worth seeing ten times. If only, she thought, there were men like him in Weatherfield but since the GIs had gone it was mostly young lads and granddads who were left and the odd serviceman on leave. Girls didn't have much choice now.

She looked at the clock. Half past six. Her friend Dot Greenhalgh (Dot Todd that was, before her marriage) would be knocking for her at seven and Vera Sharples was due at half past to keep an eye on the kids.

The tin bath was ready in front of the fire but Elsie still shivered as she took off her work clothes. She'd just soaped herself with her last bar of Lifebuoy when she heard a noise from the scullery. Her back door was always open but she wasn't expecting Dot for another fifteen minutes at least. Sod it! she thought. If anyone comes in now they either wash my back or take a running jump. No one did appear and the slight scrambling sound worried her only for a moment – just a cat on the scrounge.

She was out of the bath and half dressed when Dot yelled, 'Hiya,' as she appeared in the back room. Elsie, Dot Greenhalgh and her sister Sally Hart worked together. They all had men in their lives, but not in Weatherfield, and their attitude was that they were young and what their men didn't know couldn't hurt them. Dot had just married Walter Greenhalgh, a factory fitter now overseas, but she didn't pine for him. 'It's like 'e's on the back-burner,' she once said to Elsie. 'And that's where 'e'll stay till 'e comes 'ome for good.' Sally had married Ollie Hart, a US serviceman, in the summer and had been three-months pregnant then. Now she was blooming.

Dot began humming and did a little dance with her hands behind her back as she watched Elsie slipping on her blouse. 'It worked,' she said.

'What did?' asked Elsie.

'The notes we sent.'

The week before they'd hidden notes in the pockets of the uniforms they machined at Elliston's. It relieved the boredom and they liked to outwit the chargehand. 'Wotcha got?' asked Elsie, noticing now that Dot was hiding something.

'Close your eyes, Elsie, and 'old out your 'ands.'

Elsie laughed. 'It's not summat 'orrible, is it?'

'Well, it's not a dead rat.'

Dot put the parcel into Elsie's hands. Excitedly Elsie tore it open. 'Bloody 'ell,' she said. 'Nylons and butter. I've not tasted butter in ages. What's 'is name, then?'

Dot shrugged her shoulders. ''Ow should I know?'

'What? No note?'

Suddenly they were both laughing so much that Elsie nearly fell back into the still full tin bath. They were still laughing as they emptied it down the drain in the backyard.

When Elsie tried to share the treasures, Dot shook her head. 'The notes were your idea. What a bloody nerve you've got, askin' for little luxuries to be left at your back door. The bloke who left this little lot is probably a lunatic. Perhaps you should bolt your back gate.'

'Nah,' said Elsie. 'Who locks anything round 'ere? 'E was just a sex-starved sailor.'

'Or a soldier or an airman. We put in nearly as many notes as stitches.'

'Look, Dot, share and share alike – you 'ave 'alf this butter.'

'You keep it,' she insisted. 'Give it to the kids. Sally gets stuff from Ollie, and 'e earns more than your Arnold.'

Elsie sat down and pulled up the nylons, fixed the suspenders, then slipped on her highest heels. 'I'm in the mood to meet some lads tonight,' she said, doing a twirl. 'Then they could take us all dancin' tomorrow night.'

'Don't forget Sally's a married woman, and she looks pregnant now.'

'She 'asn't let that worry 'er so far,' said Elsie, as she admired the length of leg she was showing in her shiny nylons. 'As far as my 'usband's concerned, I 'ope I never clap eyes on 'im again.'

Half an hour later, Vera Sharples arrived looking flustered. 'I 'aven't told me mam I'm 'ere 'cos my Bob's coming round. Is that all right?'

''Course it is,' said Elsie, slipping on her coat. 'Don't go doin' owt I wouldn't do, will you?'

Vera nodded solemnly.

'And 'elp yourself to a bit of butter, pet,' said Elsie, at the back door.

'Where did you get that from?' asked Vera, wide eyed.

'A secret admirer,' said Dot.

'Oo, eh,' murmured Vera.

'You've got your Bob,' said Elsie. ''E's like a secret admirer.'

45

'I s'pose 'e is,' murmured Vera thoughtfully. 'Ta-ra then.'

Outside it was perishing cold but they hardly noticed. 'That Vera's a cartridge short of a gun load,' said Dot, as she linked arms with Elsie.

'She's all right. Just a bit soft. Ena tried to stop her growin' up so she's a bit young for her age.'

Dot laughed, 'Not like us, is she?'

Elsie grinned back. 'No, but I'm doin' me best with 'er.'

The queue, mostly of young lads, was moving quickly. 'You girls gonna sit with us?' one asked.

'Nah,' said Elsie. 'Thanks, lads, but we're fixed up.'

'Are we?' asked Dot.

Elsie had seen a couple of soldiers join the queue. One had winked at her. 'Not yet, but we soon will be.'

The cinema was nearly full, and in the darkness Elsie and Dot became separated from their quarry by a pretty usherette with a torch. Soldiers came before civilians and they were given the best seats near the back. The girls peered into the darkness and eventually found two side seats near the front. 'Too bloody close to the screen,' complained Elsie. 'I'll 'ave neck ache in the morning.'

'You'll 'ave your throat cut if you don't be quiet,' said an irate voice behind them.

The film was already half-way through, and during the interval, as Elsie queued for a cup of squash, one of the soldiers whispered in her ear, 'Fancy a drink later, sweetheart?'

Elsie looked him up and down. He was tall, pale and skinny. She preferred his mate, who was stockier and had a cheeky grin. 'Just a quick one then. Our mams are expecting us home.'

He looked slightly disappointed but winked at her. 'See you out front then – ten o'clock.'

They came out at five past ten to find the lads waiting in the foyer. 'I'm Ted,' said the tall thin one. 'And he's George.'

Before Elsie could blink she was walking arm in arm with Ted, and he was trying to nibble her ear. 'Give over,' she said, irritated that she'd ended up with the skinny one. 'I said we'd 'ave a drink with you but I didn't say owt about chewin' me ear.'

Ted wasn't easily put off. 'You're the best-lookin' girl I've seen round 'ere. Me and George are goin' back to base tomorrow

47

and then we're off to God knows where. I think you should try and be nice to us.'

Elsie didn't like him or his tone, and now they were outside it was as dark as a coal shed and she began to wonder if she hadn't made a mistake. Coronation Street seemed a long way away and she could hear that Dot was having trouble.

'If you must know,' she was saying loudly, 'I'm a married woman.'

'Don't worry me, love,' said George. 'Means you've 'ad a bit of experience. I like a lass who knows what she's doing.'

Elsie tried to think of a plan of action but Ted was fumbling with her coat buttons. 'It's bloody freezin',' she yelled. 'Don't do that!' She slapped his hand away but he took that as a playful invitation and tried to grope her breasts. As they turned into Rosamund Street she remembered that someone kept an Alsatian in a kennel in their yard.

'Come down 'ere,' she said, pulling him into the back alley, 'but keep quiet.'

Elsie wasn't sure which yard held the dog but at least she was expecting it and Ted wasn't. Suddenly the dog heard them and barked ferociously. Ted was thrown off guard and Elsie kneed him hard between the legs then added a kick on the shins for good measure. She wasn't sure where Dot was in the dark but she screamed, 'Run, Dot, run!'

She ran, the dog carried on barking and then the air-raid siren sounded. Dot caught up with her in Coronation Street and they carried on running until they reached No. 11, breathless and laughing. The siren wailed on but just as Elsie got out her key the all-clear sounded.

They were still laughing when they got inside. 'You two look as if you've 'ad a good time,' Vera said. 'Thank God the all-clear's sounded.'

'Yes,' said Elsie, still laughing. 'Thank Gawd for that.'

CHAPTER FOUR

Autumn 1943: The Island of Corsica is Taken by the French Resistance

Business at the Rovers had been brisk. A few Weatherfield servicemen had managed to get forty-eight-hour passes and the single men had spent their wages at the Rovers, for which Annie was grateful. She was also grateful for the help of young Teresa Dakins – her new nanny. According to Ena Sharples, she was 'thinner than a stick of liquorice'. Annie had insisted Teresa wore a navy dress with a white apron, which made her look more like a waitress than a nanny. 'I'll look upon it as a penance, Mrs Walker,' she said, in her soft Irish accent.

Teresa had her own room at the Rovers, which she'd decorated with religious pictures. She went to Mass on Sunday, never asked for time off, and Billy's behaviour had improved so much that Annie was both amazed and delighted. How Teresa had managed it Annie didn't know. When she asked, the girl's thin little face lit up and beneath her thick glasses her brown eyes twinkled. 'Just one of God's little miracles,' she said. 'He performs them all the time, even when we don't see them.'

Now that she had help with the children Annie's life improved. She'd been to a concert and to supper with John Barnstable. Both times his mother had been there. Annie had found the old lady difficult. She was short and round with sharp eyes, deaf when it suited her and she talked in a loud voice. Once when John had gone to fetch their coats Mrs Ivy Barnstable had leaned across and said loudly in Annie's ear, 'You're not a patch on his last girlfriend. She had real class. You just run a nasty little pub.'

Shocked, Annie said sharply, 'My public house is certainly not nasty. It's a pleasant refuge – and I'm not your son's girlfriend, I'm a married woman.' As the old woman stared at her Annie added primly, 'We are just friends. I can promise you that.'

'Aye,' said Mrs Barnstable. 'And Hitler signed a piece of paper promising not to invade Poland.'

Annie wrote to John telling him that in view of his mother's attitude it might be better if they didn't see each other again. He wrote back saying his mother was jealous of any friends he had, male or female, and he didn't want to lose her friendship. Would she meet him on Saturday for lunch in Manchester? His mother would not be there. He would wait for her at the railway station between twelve and twelve thirty.

It was Thursday and still Annie didn't know what to do.

Ena Sharples was first in the Snug. Rain was falling in torrents and she was glad to see a roaring fire. 'I'm glad to see you braved the weather, Mrs Sharples,' said Annie.

'Couldn't do owt else. I've got a bone to pick with Martha and Minnie.'

'What have they been up to?' asked Annie, as she poured Ena's milk stout. Normally Ena would have waited until she'd given her friends a dressing-down but since they weren't here she told Annie Walker. 'The Mission committee,' she explained, 'wants me to run a mother's group in the evenin' for hymn practice and Bible readings and suchlike. So I gets everythin' ready and not a Christian soul turns up.'

'Oh dear,' murmured Annie.

'You don't sound surprised.'

Annie looked round her near-empty pub. 'It's inclement weather, Mrs Sharples, and most mothers are very busy.'

'They shouldn't be too busy for the Lord. And I know for a fact there's two who promised to come and didn't.'

'I think this is the pair of them now,' said Annie, with a nod.

Ena turned towards the door as Minnie and Martha, soaked through, walked in. 'I want words with you two.'

'It was all my fault, Ena,' said Minnie, as she shook her coat over the old newspapers Mrs Walker had provided around the coat stand. 'There's no need to blame Martha.'

'You're both grown women, although sometimes, Minnie Caldwell, I think God forgot to help you grow up like He did my Vera.'

'Well, I think He's 'elpin' her now,' said Martha.

'What the 'eck do you mean by that, Martha Longhurst?'

'You're always sayin' the Good Lord moves in mysterious ways.'

'And what if I am? Explain yerself.'

Martha shrugged. 'Just that your Vera's been seen goin' in and out of Elsie Tanner's at all times of night. And I've 'eard that Bob

Lomax has been with her.'

'How dare you! My Vera's a good girl. She may be slow but she's been brought up in a good Christian home.'

'Well, it seems she prefers Elsie Tanner's heathen ways.'

Ena plonked herself down and sipped her milk stout as if it had the medicinal qualities of brandy.

'Don't upset yourself, Ena,' said Minnie. 'Martha and me was plannin' to come to the mission but I've got a bit of bother at home.'

'Don't talk in riddles, woman. What's all this got to do with my Vera?'

'Nothin' at all, Ena. As you said, Vera's a good girl. But I asked Martha to listen for me.'

Ena's glance at Minnie would have withered an irate camel but Minnie carried on nervously. 'As I said to Martha, if anyone can sort this out it'll be Ena.'

Ena's expression softened. 'Stop goin' round 'ouses, Minnie, and tell me what's up.'

Minnie eased herself to the edge of her seat. 'Ena, I've bin 'earin' noises for days now. I thought I'd gone doo-lally. Mam didn't 'ear anything.'

'Your mam is as deaf as a tin 'elmet.'

'Please, Ena, let me finish. My Mabel 'ears things no one else does and 'er 'ackles and 'er fur kept goin' on end. So I asks Martha to come in the 'ouse and listen for me.'

'And?'

'She didn't 'ear anything. We 'ad to wait, you see. The noises seem to come at night. And I reckon it's ... I reckon it's a ghost.'

'You're barmy, Minnie Caldwell. Your Armistead would be ashamed of you. Some daft ideas you do come up with. And 'ow come you didn't 'ear anything, Martha Longhurst? You could 'ear a whisper of gossip in an empty barn.'

Martha sniffed. 'I've never known *you* to refuse to listen to a bit of gossip.'

'That's as maybe,' said Ena, glaring at her. 'But Minnie 'ere is vergin' on going "up top road" so we'd better do summat before they come to take her away.'

The local mental hospital was 'up top road' and by now Minnie was near to tears. 'Call yourself a Christian woman, Ena?' she said. 'I'm right worried an' all you can do is mek fun of me.'

'You're always worried over summat, Minnie Caldwell, so take that look off your face or you'll turn the beer.'

Minnie muttered, 'I'm not stayin' 'ere to

be insulted. I 'eard what I 'eard.' Then, with a glower at both Ena and Martha, she stood up, walked to the coat-stand, grabbed her coat and walked out without even putting it round her shoulders.

'That was right nasty, Ena,' said Martha. 'If you won't 'elp her, what's she goin' to do?'

'I didn't say I wouldn't 'elp her. I'll manage another milk stout and then get meself round to Minnie's for a vigil. I shall stay all night or until I 'ear summat. Ghosts! I've an idea the only ghosts she's got is a bird in the attic or mice under the floor-boards.'

'I 'ate mice,' said Martha, shuddering.

'Don't expect they'd want to share your billet, Martha Longhurst. You wouldn't 'ave enough scraps to feed a cockroach.'

Twenty minutes later Ena was banging on Minnie's door. 'There's no need to knock so 'ard, Ena,' said a flustered Minnie, as she opened the door. 'Bangin' like that won't frighten ghosts away.'

'There's no such things as ghosts, and well you know it.'

'You'd better come in, Ena,' said Minnie, looking tearful. 'And I do believe in ghosts. What about angels and the Holy Ghost? I

56

tek it you believe in them?'

Ena marched into the back room and surveyed the scene. Minnie kept a clean and tidy home. She was fond of lace, and there was a lace runner on the drop-leaf table and lace antimacassars on the two armchairs. Although the lino was worn she'd made two rag rugs to cover the worst bits and for Mabel to sit on in front of the fire.

Ena slipped off her coat and handed it to Minnie. Then she sat in the chair nearest the fire. 'The Holy Ghost isn't a *real* ghost, Minnie,' she said. ''E's a good spirit, not a lost soul frightenin' folk to death.'

Minnie hung up Ena's coat and shook a few more lumps of coal from the scuttle on to the fire.

'You'd best put kettle on, then,' said Ena, picking up the poker to give the coals a helping hand. 'We'll see if your ghost wants to come out to play tonight.'

Minnie wondered if a ghost could be scared, like mortals. Because she had a feeling that Ena had it in her to scare anyone dead or alive – even 'Itler.

An hour later Minnie hadn't heard a sound. 'I've got a feelin' you may 'ave done the trick, Ena.'

'Too soon to say that, Minnie Caldwell. At

first light we should bloomin' well know.'

'Are you stayin' up all night Ena?'

'Yes by 'eck, and you're stayin' with me.'

Minnie sighed and walked towards the door. 'I'll get some blankets, then.'

'And pillows. May as well be comfortable as we wait for our ghostie.'

'I do wish you'd take it seriously, Ena.'

'I'm 'ere ain't I? And God's on our side.'

'If you say so, Ena.'

At No. 11, Elsie had planned to get some ironing done but it was nearly ten o'clock and she hadn't even started. Once she'd got the kids to bed she'd sat down and fallen asleep. It had been a rotten day at the factory, the boiler had packed up and they'd had to work in their coats.

Dot had said she'd pop round at about ten so Elsie had planed to do some ironing before she came, but all she'd managed to do so far was heat up the flat-iron.

This time when she heard a noise she was quick, but not quick enough. All she could see in the dark outside was the twinkle of raindrops on the back of a tall man as he disappeared through the yard door. On the back step he'd placed three brown-paper parcels. She gathered them up, put them on the table and waited excitedly for Dot to turn up.

Within seconds Dot had appeared. 'Did you see him?' asked Elsie.

'See who? What are you talkin' about?'

Elsie pointed to the parcels on the table. 'Oh, my Gawd,' said Dot. 'Has he just been?'

''E probably passed you in the street.'

'Must be a bloody phantom then 'cos I didn't see a soul.'

Elsie could wait no longer. ''Ere, you open one,' she said, handing the biggest parcel to Dot. 'It might be more butter.'

Dot began tearing at the brown paper. 'It's better than Christmas, this is.' Inside was a small bottle of brandy, a bottle of 'Evening in Paris' perfume and a jar of Pond's Cold Cream. Elsie's packages contained a huge hunk of cheese, a bottle of Camp coffee and a two-pound bag of sugar.

'Gawd, Elsie, this must be black-market stuff. We'd better be careful.'

'Who's gonna find out about it? We 'aven't even seen 'im.'

Dot fondled the brandy bottle. 'There could be more than one bloke. And in this life you never get owt for nowt. He just wants to get into your knickers.'

'Well 'e'll find enough room,' laughed

Elsie. 'All me knickers need new elastic.'

Dot looked serious. ''E doesn't know you, does 'e? I mean, nothin' gets left at my door.'

'Nah. 'Ow would he know me? 'E just thinks 'e's on to a good thing. 'E must be desperate.'

'Or just a barmy bugger.'

'Well 'e must 'ave some brass to buy this lot.'

For a few moments they stood silently contemplating their treasures until Dot started sniffing. 'There's an 'orrible smell in 'ere, Elsie.'

'Oh bloody 'ell – it's me iron. It's been on the gas for ages.' She ran into the scullery and grabbed a tea cloth. The iron looked black on the bottom and it was red hot. 'Time for a drink, Dot. Sod the ironin'. 'Ow d'you fancy a cup of Camp with brandy?'

'Elsie, I haven't 'ad a brandy in years. Sounds smashin' to me.'

They sat and drank until the brandy bottle was empty and everything they said made them laugh. They laughed most about Ted and George. 'You should 'ave seen 'is face, Dot, when I kneed him in the nuts. I don't know what surprised 'im more, the dog barkin' or me 'armin' his essentials.'

Elsie laughed again. 'We'll never find out now, will we?'

'No, thank Gawd. Ugly beggars, weren't they?'

'It were too dark to see.'

'Just as bloody well.'

As she staggered home Dot was still smiling. She caught a glimpse of a man's shape ahead of her in the darkness but she didn't take any notice. The rain was still falling but she didn't take any notice of that either.

Tucked up under blankets Ena and Minnie slept in snatches. When Ena woke she made sure she wasn't alone. 'Minnie Caldwell, I 'aven't 'eard as much as a breath of wind in the bloomin' chimney.' Minnie, half-asleep, only grunted. With Ena for company she'd relaxed, believing any ghost would keep his or her distance.

It was nearly three a.m. when Ena woke again. She'd been dreaming of her dead husband Alfred and she felt bleary-eyed and not quite awake. But she'd heard something, and she would have sworn on the Bible that the gas lamps flickered at the same time as she heard the footsteps and a low moaning sound. 'Minnie, wake up. I've 'eard summat.'

'What's 'appened? What's to do?' Minnie sat bolt upright, rubbing her eyes.

'I'm not sure where it's coming from.'

Minnie couldn't help noticing the slight change in Ena's voice.

'You're not scared, are you, Ena?'

'Don't be so daft. I'm scared of nowt. But your Mabel's 'eard something.'

The cat was crouched on her haunches wide-eyed with terror. Minnie eased herself up from the chair and approached Mabel, but she was too fast and leaped away to cower under the table. 'Ooh, Ena, what are we going to do?'

'We'll keep our 'eads, that's what we'll do.'

'You've gone ever so pale, Ena, as white as Mabel's paws.'

'Stop mitherin', Minnie Caldwell, and listen.'

They both listened. The dying fire crackled in the grate and the gas lamps hissed softly but otherwise the noise had stopped. 'It wasn't mice I 'eard,' said Ena, 'or even bats.'

Minnie shuddered. 'It is a ghost, Ena, isn't it? I've got no 'oles in me slates and me attic 'as only got a tiny little trap door. Nobody could get through it.'

'I don't want to say you're right, Minnie,

but that wailin' noise didn't sound 'uman.'

'You think it *is* a ghost, then?'

Ena shrugged. 'There's more in 'eaven and earth than folk like us know about. I'm thinkin' we might need someone who'd know more about it than we do.'

'Who are you thinking of, Ena?'

'Mr Swindley. 'E'll know. 'E may not be much of a preacher but 'e'll 'elp us on ghosts. 'E'll say the right prayers and sing the right hymns.'

Minnie shook her head. 'I think we'll need a proper vicar for this with a dog collar and everythin'.'

'A chapel man is what we need, Minnie. We'll 'ave no hoity-toity church vicars in 'ere.'

'If you say so, Ena. What will Mr Swindley *do?*'

'I've just told you that. Now, let's get back to sleep. If it is a ghost it ain't goin' to ravish you in your sleep. Ghosts don't 'ave them sort of ideas.'

Minnie snuggled down beneath the blankets. 'I'd never thought of that, Ena.'

'Well, you wouldn't, would you, Minnie? Now, go to sleep and stop mitherin'.'

During the last few weeks Sally Hart had

63

grown and grown, and her mother, Vi, had let out as many of her clothes as she could. 'I never showed at all till I was seven months gone,' Sally said to Dot, as they sat in the kitchen of No. 9, 'but now I feel like I've got a bag of cement up me jumper.'

'You're like a barrage balloon,' said Dot, laughing, 'but you're near your time so you'll be doing no dancin' for a while.'

'You will stay with me, Dot, if there's a raid, won't you?' said Sally, grabbing her sister's hand.

'Give over, Sally. Mam and me won't leave you for a second if the bombs are as near as Rosamund Street and falling like ruddy confetti.'

Sally managed a weak smile. She'd got terrible backache and she fidgeted on the hard wooden carver chair her dad usually sat in.

A few minutes later Vi came in with a loaf of bread and a pound of liver under her arm. 'That's grand, that is,' she said irritably, 'you two doin' nothin' while I've been queuing for hours. Get the irons on the stove. There's enough ironing to keep you two goin' all evenin'. I've got tea to cook and a pile of mendin' and since neither of you can thread a bloomin' needle...'

'Don't go on, Mam,' said Dot. 'Sally looks a bit peaky.'

Vi cast a quick glance at Sally. 'She's not due yet,' she said, as if Sally wasn't there. 'I reckon she's got 'er dates wrong. She don't look near big enough to me. I bet the 'ead's not down far enough yet.'

While Vi peeled potatoes and chopped cabbage Dot set two flat-irons to heat up. 'Don't forget to rub a bit o' soap on them,' said Vi. 'I don't want them iron marks on my clothes.'

'You're not ailin', Mam, are you?' asked Dot. 'You look ever so tired.'

Vi smoothed back some stray grey hairs from her forehead. 'What yer mean is I'm in a bad mood. Well, I am. Someone I know 'ad a cot for sale in Rosamund Street and when I got there it'd gone.'

'Never mind, Mam, we'll manage,' said Dot. 'We've got the drawer emptied from the press so we can mek do.'

Vi sighed. 'That's all I've ever done, mek do. I was 'opin' my first grandchild would at least 'ave a cot.'

'Mam,' Sally's plaintive voice came from the back room. 'I've got a bit o' backache.'

'So 'ave I, pet,' said Vi. 'You get on with the ironin'. It'll tek your mind off yer back.'

Sally struggled to her feet and soon had to admit that Vi was right. Standing up she did feel a bit better. Dot gave her a few hankies to iron while she folded sheets, and Vi grumbled in the scullery about the quality of the liver. ''Urry up, you two,' Vi called, after they'd been ironing for half an hour. 'I want to get tea cooked an' on the table.'

Dot rolled her eyes. With Vi in this mood they just couldn't win.

Once the ironing had been put away Dot laid the table and Sally resumed her place in the carver chair. ''Itch yerself up,' said Dot, as she slipped a cushion on the seat. Sally smiled with relief at the comfort. Vi had dished up liver, mashed potatoes and onions with gravy so thick it would have plugged sinks. Sally looked at her plate and felt sick. Her mother was a terrible cook. Blood was oozing from the liver and mixing with the lumpy gravy.

'Tek that look off your face, Sally,' said Vi. 'You needs to keep up your strength.'

Sally picked up her knife and fork and started on the cabbage. She looked across at Dot and winked at her. Dot knew what to do. 'Mam, is there any bread?' she asked.

'There's always bread, Dot,' said Vi, 'as

you well know, but don't you go cuttin' it. You cut bread like a lumberjack. I'll do it.'

Once Vi had left the table Dot grabbed a piece of old newspaper destined to be torn into squares for the privy, wrapped the liver in it and thrust it into her handbag. Sally smiled with relief. When the bread appeared she ate a slice and said, 'That were nice, Mam, but I'm full now.'

Vi looked disapprovingly at the left-over vegetables. 'You eat too much bread, Sally, but you can mek a bit o' space for a nice rice pudding.'

Sally felt like crying – her stomach was gripping and griping and her back hurt like someone was punching her. She heaved at the thought of her mother's rice pudding – she always got the skin and she hated that brown burnt bit.

Then, just as Sally thought she couldn't feel worse, she felt a gush of warm water trickle down her leg. The shame of it. She hadn't known she wanted to go, she'd had no warning. Mam would be cross about the cushion. Perhaps if she stayed put Vi need not know what had happened.

Sally struggled through a few mouthfuls of rice pudding, then Vi went out to start the washing up and Dot finished the rest.

'I've wet meself,' Sally whispered to Dot. 'I can't seem to stop going.'

'I'll 'ide the cushion,' Dot whispered back. 'You go and sort yerself out.'

A few minutes later Sally came back, looking ashen. 'I'm bleedin',' she said, as she sat down in her dad's chair. Then she gripped the arms as a spasm of pain took her breath away.

'Mam! Mam!' yelled Dot. 'Our Sally's bin tekken poorly.'

Vi rushed in, took one look at her daughter and knew. 'Our Sally's not poorly. It's her time.'

At that moment the air raid siren wailed. Sally clung to Vi's arm. 'I'm scared. Don't leave me, will you?'

Vi laughed. 'We'd like as leave you as a pigeon fancier would shut his birds out. Now then, Dot, you can put kettle on.'

'What for, Mam?'

'A brew, what do you think? We'll be a good few hours yet.'

Sally refused to leave the chair for her bed. 'I don't want to lie down, Mam. If we get bombed I'll 'ave to try to mek it to the shelter.'

'You won't be able, pet. You just concentrate on 'avin' this baby.'

'I wet meself, Mam,' admitted Sally. 'On your best cushion.'

'Yer didn't wet yourself, pet,' said Vi, patting her daughter's hand. 'That was your waters breakin' – don't yer know nowt?'

Sally relaxed in the chair. Her mam seemed to know what she was doing and she felt a lot better now she knew she hadn't disgraced herself. The pains began to come every ten minutes or so but Vi got Dot to rub her sister's back hard with the heel of her hand right at the base of her spine and that helped.

An hour or so after the air raid warning they heard low rumblings in the distance. 'Nothin' to fret about,' said Vi. 'That's Manchester gettin' it. I've a feelin' in me bones it won't come Weatherfield way tonight.'

'I 'ope you're right.'

Sally was still in labour when the all-clear sounded at midnight. Dot felt near to tears on her sister's behalf. Sally was sweating and red in the face, and sometimes she cried out with the pain in her back. ''Ow much longer, Mam?' she asked.

Vi looked at her younger daughter sternly. 'A babby takes nine months to grow and they don't shell like peas

69

whatever you 'ear 'bout women who only tek a couple of hours. Our Sally's goin' sure and steady and that's the best way. Too fast, and it's bad for the babby. Now, don't start shrikin', get that drawer out and put best towels on the bottom and a hottie underneath with a little vest, nightie and nappy warmin' up on it.'

Dot filled the stone hot-water bottle and took it upstairs. When she looked at the makeshift cot she found it hard to believe that perhaps by morning a new little person would be lying there.

When she came downstairs things had changed. Sally was grunting and trying to swear at the same time and now she was lying on the floor with her skirt up, no knickers and her legs wide open. 'There's nowt dignified about 'avin' a baby, is there?' said Dot, who had only the vaguest idea about childbirth.

'Yer dignity's the last thing to worry about,' said Vi. 'Now, Dot, you 'old her shoulders and I'll deal with other end.'

Sally could hardly think now. Something sharp was stabbing at her back and she knew she was making grunting noises. She couldn't go on, she was convinced of that. 'When I see the 'ead you can push, pet,' said

Vi. 'You're doin' reet well now. It won't be long.'

Dot, holding Sally, had pins and needles in her feet, and every time Sally moaned she wanted to moan too. It seemed to go on and on.

'I can see the 'ead, our Sally,' encouraged Vi, who now had beads of sweat on her forehead. 'Nearly there, love.'

Sally pushed and grunted and grew redder in the face. An hour passed. Vi began to frown. 'Dot, I'll 'old 'er while you fetch pillows and towels and get a saucepan on the boil.'

Vi took over Dot's position and Dot stood stamping her feet to get rid of her pins and needles. 'Not bloody Christmas – now!' yelled Vi. Dot looked anxiously at her mother. Until now Vi had seemed confident but Dot sensed something had gone wrong and with a final worried glance at her sister she ran upstairs and began grabbing pillows and towels. In her hurry she nearly fell down the steep stairs. 'Don't break your neck,' said Vi. 'I might need yer to find a doctor.'

Vi banked Sally up with pillows, placed the clean towels under her bottom and one across her belly, then gave her some water to

71

drink. Dot put a saucepan of cold water on to boil then stood awaiting instructions. Sally, meanwhile, was groaning and seemed weak. 'You 'ang on Sally,' shouted Dot.

'There's no need to shout at 'er. She can still 'ear.'

'Mam, help me,' said Sally weakly.

'I'm goin' to, pet. Not long now.' Vi stood up, pushed Dot into the scullery and whispered, 'Get a doctor 'ere – quick!' She pressed a torch into Dot's hand. 'Look where you're going. It'll be black as a coalman's boot out there.'

And it was. The dark engulfed Dot. She half ran, half walked, hoping to see an ARP warden or a policeman but the street was deserted. She ran on to the Glad Tidings Mission Hall and banged several times on the door.

In moments, Ena Sharples appeared wearing a man's dressing gown and with curlers in her hair. 'By 'eck, Dot Green-halgh, you're a noisy one.' Then, seeing the girl's expression, Ena asked, 'What's 'appened?'

'It's our Sally – she's 'avin' baby and summat's wrong. She needs the doctor.'

'You get back 'ome. I'll get doctor. There's a fire on the outskirts of Weatherfield and 'e'll most likely be there.'

Dot hesitated.

'Go on, girl. Run! You tell your mam I'll get 'im if I 'as to drag 'im there by 'is braces.'

Dot arrived home breathless. She took one look at her mother's face and then at Sally. 'She's gone all pale, Mam.'

'Where's the doc?'

'Ena Sharples is goin' for 'im. She says 'e's at a fire.'

'I'll wait no more than fifteen minutes. Our Sally's been pushin' two an 'alf hours.'

'What do we do, Mam, if doctor doesn't come?'

Vi put a finger to her lips and whispered. 'I'll do summat, don't you worry.'

'Oh, gawd, you're not goin' cut 'er belly open?' cried Dot in horror.

'Don't be daft, girl, and keep your voice down.'

Dot really didn't want to know *what* her mother was going to do. She felt sick.

'Give our Sally a little warm water and sugar and a drop of brandy in it.'

Dot found the emergency half-bottle of brandy in the front-parlour sideboard and took a swig herself before mixing Sally's drink. Then she sat on the floor and put the cup to Sally's lips. The brandy seemed to give her the strength and during the next pushing session she shouted out, 'Never again! I'll 'ave nowt to do with a man ever again.' When the pain passed she lay back exhausted on the pillows and murmured. 'I want my Ollie.'

'Now, listen 'ere and listen good, our Sal,' said Vi firmly. 'The doc ain't arrived so you've got to do what I say. You pushes when I tells you and not before. Dot 'ere will 'old yer legs. If yer wants to 'oller you can.'

'What are you goin' to do, Mam?' murmured Sally.

'I'm going to 'elp you, that's all yer needs to know.'

'I wish my Ollie was 'ere,' said Sally again.

'Thank Gawd 'e isn't,' said Vi. ''E'd be as much use as a torch to a blind man.'

Vi washed her hands carefully with Sunlight soap, picked up a pair of scissors then took a deep breath. She was scared witless. She knelt on the floor and saw the expression on Dot's face. 'You just tek care of our Sal and tek no notice of me.'

Dot closed her eyes and Vi wished she could close hers too.

When the next contractions came it was

fierce and Sally screamed out, 'Oh, Gawd, Mam! Oh, Gawd!'

'Start 'ollering, pet,' she said. 'You can push now for all you're worth.'

Seconds later Vi breathed, 'Thank Gawd for that.' She knew now the next push would do it. 'Come on, my sweetheart, nearly there.'

Sally pushed as if her life depended on it. Then, gloriously, the pain was over and she raised her head in time to see her baby's face just as the little mouth took its first gasp. She sank back. 'Oo, Mam,' she murmured.

Vi laid the baby on Sally's chest and covered him with a towel. 'What is it, Mam?'

Vi laughed. 'Oh, 'eck. I forgot to look.' She lifted the towel to check. 'It's a boy, and 'e's bloody perfect.' Vi could feel the tears of relief and joy running down her cheeks. It was the best moment of her whole life.

Sally smiled in tired contentment as the baby rooted for her breast.

Neither she nor Vi noticed that Dot had fainted.

Moments later an elderly doctor they had never seen before came in with Ena Sharples leading the way. He cut the cord.

'Grand job you've done, Mrs Todd. I couldn't have done better myself.' Vi swelled with pride, and after she'd paid him five shillings, he left. They quickly washed 'our Clark' and dressed him in his white nightie and cardigan. Ena made a brew and hot toast with dripping, and after three slices and hot sweet tea Sally's colour returned to normal.

'You don't mind 'im bein' called Clark, do you, Mam?' asked Sally drowsily.

'As long as 'e's not called Adolf,' said Vi, 'I'm 'appy.'

Her grandson soon nestled and fell asleep beside his proud mother and Vi added brandy liberally to her tea, Ena's and Dot's.

Dot still felt a bit shaky and was sorry to have missed the birth, but she was thrilled that Sally looked more like her old self – and as for 'our Clark' she could only look at him in wonderment. 'He's champion, Mam,' she said. 'Look at his 'air and 'is little fingers.'

'Aye,' said Vi. ''E's smashin'. I'm right proud of our Sal for bein' so brave.'

'It was you what 'elped her, Vi,' said Ena. And then, feeling she had to add a touch of realism to the event, said, 'Your Sally will 'ave her work cut out now.'

But nothing Ena Sharples said at that

moment could alter the sheer happiness of the Todd family. 'A beautiful baby boy,' said Vi proudly, before swigging back a neat brandy. 'And he's my grandson.'

CHAPTER FIVE

Winter 1943: First Major Daylight Raid on Berlin

Ida Barlow read and re-read the letter. She'd had a postcard at Christmas from Frank, a standard issue POW card telling her that he was well. But now she had a letter and every word was precious. He was keeping busy, was glad the winter was nearly over and he was grateful for the Red Cross parcels they received. He said how much he missed his family and that he was sure the war would be over soon. She was to be brave and keep her chin up.

Bessie was as excited as Ida about the letter. 'That's lovely for you, pet. Just you look on the bright side – at least as a POW 'e won't be fightin' any more. 'E'll come 'ome to you safe and sound.' Somehow that didn't cheer Ida up. What would he be like when he came home?

'Now, come on, Ida,' said Bessie briskly, 'tek that face off yer. I've got some lovely bottled fruit for you. That'll cheer you up.'

Ida managed a smile as she hugged Bessie. 'I feel as if I'm always taking food from you and Albert.'

'Albert don't go short. You can tell that by the size of 'im.'

Ida smiled. ''E's a fine figure of a man – 'e's like Mr Churchill.'

''E'd like to run country, that's for sure.'

Bessie made a pot of tea while Ida woke David from his nap in the armchair. He snuggled, eyes still closed, on her lap. ''E's a little angel, isn't he?' said Bessie, as she laid down the tea tray. 'Let me 'old 'im for a while. You pour the tea and 'ave one in peace.'

Ida sat at the table deep in thought and drank her tea. 'You look worried, pet,' said Bessie. 'What's up?'

'It's Kenneth. He's a strange little lad. When I talk about his dad he doesn't look a bit pleased.'

'And you don't know why?'

Ida shook her head.

''E's jealous.'

'Of his own dad?' queried Ida, in amazement.

Bessie nodded. 'I've seen it before in the first war. Eldest boys like your Kenneth forget they're nowt but babes and start actin' like little men. 'Ow many times have you called 'im "your little man"?'

Ida thought about that. 'I s'pose you're right, Bessie.'

'I'm right,' said Bessie firmly. 'And I bet both the babbies sleep in your bed at night.'

Ida nodded. 'They don't sleep well on their own, Bessie. They start off in their own beds but what with the raids and everything they get scared.'

'You're not the only one who sleeps with their kiddies,' said Bessie. 'It's only natural in times like these. But then one day out of the blue a big stranger in uniform comes and 'e gets in bed with their mam. What must they think?'

'But 'e's their father.'

'That's as maybe, but they don't know each other, do they?'

Ida stared into her teacup as David struggled from Bessie's lap and toddled across the room to join her. 'What do I do about it, Bessie?'

'Nowt you can do, really. When your Frank does come 'ome 'e'll be jealous too. 'E'll want you all to 'imself and 'e'll want a bit o' peace.'

Ida looked even more worried now.

'Stop your frettin',' said Bessie. 'On Frank's first night back we'll 'ave the kids – give you a chance to be with Frank on yer own. And let's 'ope that day won't be far away.'

'Won't Albert mind?'

Bessie laughed. 'He loves those two as if they were 'is own, so don't you worry about that.'

Ida brightened as she imagined the day Frank would return, and how it would be to cuddle up in bed with her man once more. The only niggle of doubt she had now was that he might seem like a stranger to her too.

Betty Preston's job at Earnshaw's munitions factory had come as a shock to her. The boiler-suits they wore didn't flatter her buxom figure and it didn't suit her face to have her curly hair scraped back under a headscarf. Some of the women wore curlers under their scarves and didn't care how they looked. Betty wasn't as pretty as some but she did think being presentable was important, and she always tried to look well groomed. She had expected the work to be hard but the women were even harder.

Gradually she was getting used to the bad

language and their continuous chatting about dancing and the men they'd met. It upset her that the married women seemed the worst. With their husbands away fighting, they all acted as if they were single again. Every week someone was to be found crying in the ladies' because they had been 'caught'. Most often they said their babies were premature, and with a little luck their husbands would never find them out, but one woman wasn't so lucky. Her husband had come home on leave unexpectedly and found her not only pregnant but with her boyfriend. It had nearly come to murder and both husband and boyfriend had been arrested. Betty had found it quite distressing but the women she worked with seemed to take it in their stride.

Betty had never had a boyfriend. Her father Harold was a strict God-fearing man and she'd been happy to live by his rules, but she had a mind of her own and now, at eighteen, she wanted to do what *she* wanted, not what her father thought she should do.

One Saturday evening she asked her sister Maggie to go to the pictures with her. Harold and their mother Margaret had fallen asleep by the fireside so they whispered together in the scullery. 'Come on,

Maggie, it'll be a good film. You'll enjoy it.'

Maggie looked worried. 'What if 'e finds out?'

''Ow should 'e find out? We'll say we went to see a friend.'

Nothing Betty said could make timid Maggie change her mind. 'I'll go on my own, then. You can tell him I'm baby-sittin' or summat.'

'Lyin's a sin, Betty.'

Betty shrugged. 'Well, goin' to the pictures isn't. It's our patriotic duty to watch the Pathé News.'

'Who says?'

'I do,' said Betty.

'What about Mam?'

'What about 'er?'

'What'll I give 'er to eat?'

'There's always bread and drippin'. You know she'll eat anything.'

Betty crept out of the house and into the fresh night air. She didn't mind the cold – she was well padded enough – and it was a relief to be away from the stifling atmosphere at home. Although she was sure she loved her mam and dad, it wasn't easy.

Betty could just about remember her mother being different. She'd been a child then and she could remember her mam

83

laughing and playing hide-and-seek with them or taking them to the Red Rec and pushing them on the swings. Then, as the years went by, she got quieter and took to eating. And she just got fatter and fatter. When the war started Betty thought she would lose weight but she didn't. Harold had insisted that both girls gave up their sugar ration for Mam, and he always seemed to find extras for her. He ate very little himself and most of his food found its way to their mother's plate.

Betty knew the neighbours called him 'Holy Harold', and he looked like a crow with his bent back and his black coat-tails flapping behind him. As for her mother, few people knew she was even alive. She hadn't left the house in years and Betty had realized as she got older that that was what her father wanted. Her mother was the queen bee who had to be fed and her dad was a worker bee who had to keep her sitting in the hive. It wasn't right, Betty thought, but what could she do?

Once she joined the cinema queue she put her family out of her mind. She wanted to enjoy herself even if she was on her own. It didn't bother her that there were mostly couples standing outside the Bijou. She was just glad to be out of her Tile Street home and mixing with folk who just wanted to enjoy themselves.

The long queue was slow-moving and people got bored. Someone started singing 'It's A Long Way to Tipperary' and she soon found herself joining in. She had a good voice – she'd even sung in the church choir before the war and she was enjoying herself so much she didn't notice the man in uniform edging nearer to her. When he began singing, too, she did notice him. He had a fine deep voice and he could sing in tune. Betty was so impressed she turned to look at his face. His face was as handsome as she'd expected from his voice, and she turned away as she blushed. When they'd finished singing he tapped her shoulder. 'You have a lovely voice.'

To Betty's ears he sounded posh. He was from down south she could tell. 'You sounded champion too,' she said.

'I'm Ted Farrell. Corporal. I'm stationed in Manchester. All on my tod and looking for a pretty girl to share the evening with.'

'You're a bold one,' said Betty, and giggled.

'Fair maiden was never won over by a chap who didn't breach the front line.'

'You talk ever so posh,' said Betty. 'You're not from round 'ere are you?'

He smiled. 'Yeah, I'm really posh. I say "barth" and "parth" and "bus". I can't quite say "boos" like the locals do. I'm from Portsmouth where they speak proper English.'

Betty couldn't let that go. 'There's nowt wrong with the way people round 'ere speak.'

'Did I say there was? Now I've met you the north is improving by the minute. It would get even better if I knew your name.'

'Betty Preston.'

'Well, pretty Betty Preston, now we've been properly introduced perhaps we could sit together to watch the picture.'

No one had ever called Betty pretty. 'Oh, all right,' she said, suddenly shy and a bit unsure. When they got to the box office he insisted on paying.

Betty could hardly concentrate on the film she was so conscious of the handsome soldier sitting beside her. Most of the Weatherfield lads were too rough for her and those who knew her wouldn't come anywhere near because of 'Holy Harold'. She resolved there and then to lie about where she lived. Since she'd worked at

86

Earnshaw's she'd learned more about the world and she realized that if her dad had his way she'd turn out like her mother. She had a feeling that Corporal Ted Farrell was going to become very special to her, and Betty wasn't going to let anyone come between them.

That night Ida Barlow and Bessie Tatlock were in the cinema. Bessie had asked Albert to baby-sit because Ida hadn't been out in the evening for weeks and she was definitely looking peaky. During the Pathé News there was a little feature on 'make do and mend' and forming neighbourhood sewing groups.

'We could do that,' whispered Bessie.

Ida didn't answer. She was thinking about Frank's last leave and wishing she could turn the clock back. Was he getting enough to eat, she wondered. He was fussy about his food and thought foreign food was ''orrible'.

'What do you think, Ida?' Bessie persisted.

'Aye. It's a good idea.'

On the way home Bessie talked non-stop. 'We could put a little notice in Mrs Foyle's shop. There's those that can't sew in the Street – the likes of Elsie Tanner for one. She might like some of her clothes altered, and Mrs Walker, she likes to be fashionable. We could charge them just a little.'

Ida nodded. She wanted to get home as quickly as possible. She wasn't used to being out after dark, socializing. She was only used to rushing to the Glad Tidings Mission Hall shelter and she had a strange feeling in the pit of her stomach – as if she was about to hear bad news.

Bessie carried a tiny torch but it was only as bright as a match in the dark. In the alleyway leading to the back door she stumbled first against a dustbin and then, in Ida's yard, her toe hit a flower-pot. They both laughed nervously. 'Do be careful, Bessie. Albert will think you've had a drink.'

Bessie chuckled. 'I can't remember last time I 'ad a drink. I reckon that was Christmas 1939. I don't like the taste of the stuff.'

Ida was about to answer when she heard a creaking sound. It was the privy door opening. 'Oh, Lor'!' shrieked Bessie, as a man appeared. In the darkness all either of them could see was a sailor's uniform. Just for a moment Ida stood open-mouthed, thinking by some miracle it was Frank. Then he spoke and she realized he was a stranger.

'Sorry, ladies,' said the sailor, moving nearer to them. 'I've been in the Rovers drinkin' with me mates and I got took short. I saw your back gate was ajar and I was desperate, if you know what I mean.'

'Where are you off to now, then?' asked Bessie.

'I'm 'oping to find a mate in Manchester. "E'll give me a bed.'

'I bet you've missed the last bus,' said Bessie. 'You can stay with us, if you like.'

He paused, but not for long. 'That's very good of you, missus. It'd be a treat.'

Ida gave him a shy smile, 'What's your name?'

'Ron – Ronald Feathers. They call me Duck in the Navy.'

Albert Tatlock looked up in surprise as they entered with a sailor in tow but he stood up and shook his hand. 'Are you hungry, lad?'

'I'm always 'ungry,' Ron said. 'Me mother couldn't cope with me appetite. I reckon that's why she wanted me to join up.'

Albert tapped out his pipe. 'That's one thing about the services, they do try to keep you stoked up. You can come next door if you like, my missus'll give you summat tasty.'

'No, I'll do it,' said Ida eagerly. 'It's nice to cook for a bit of company.'

Ida went into the kitchen with Bessie and began peeling potatoes. ''E's a nice-lookin' lad,' said Bessie. 'My Albert loves a chat with a serviceman – 'e'll keep the lad up till the early hours.'

Ida only had a little bit of cheese, bread, two slices of ham and some rice pudding in the larder. She sliced the potatoes thinly and fried them in a little square of lard. Bessie cut some bread and spread it with margarine then made a pot of tea.

Ron seemed well pleased with the food, and Ida watched him eat with satisfaction. It was a treat to cook for a man but she wished he was her Frank.

Once the Tatlocks and Ron had left, the house seemed very quiet. Ida reread Frank's letter and when she went to bed that night she kissed his photo. 'You'll soon be 'ome, pet,' she said aloud. 'Where you belong.'

Betty and Ted Farrell walked out of the Bijou into the dark and the wailing of the air-raid siren. 'It won't be much,' said Ted.

Betty laughed. ''Ave you got 'Itler's word on that?'

Ted took her hand. 'Come on, Betty, it

might only be one Luftwaffe plane but it could still finish us off. Let's run.'

'Where to?' asked Betty, out of breath after a few hundred yards.

He stopped. 'You tell me. I'm lost.'

'The Glad Tidings Mission Hall on Coronation Street – it's nearby.'

'I'm not doing any praying,' said Ted, squeezing her hand.

When they arrived Ena Sharples was already playing the harmonium. She was singing 'Onward Christian Soldiers' at the top of her voice.

Betty looked round nervously. She'd never been the subject of gossip but she might be now if one of Earnshaw's girls saw her. She knew a few people by sight but now the raids were shorter and fewer the numbers flocking to the Mission cellar had dwindled. Ida Barlow sat on a mattress with her two children, who were half asleep. Betty thought she looked as if she'd been crying. Martha Longhurst, Ena's friend, was making cups of tea and handing them round. In all there were only about eight people. Betty knew that most sheltered now under heavy tables or a Morrison shelter in their front rooms. Her own mother didn't move from her chair and Harold, believing the Lord would protect him of all people, sat beside her, praying loudly so that God would hear him above the drone of the Stukas.

Ted found a spare mattress and they sat down together and joined in with the singing. He put an arm around Betty's shoulders and she didn't mind a bit.

She felt quite sorry when the all-clear sounded half an hour later.

CHAPTER SIX

Winter 1943: The Russians Enter Romania

'Minnie Caldwell's ghost is summat like the war,' Ena said, as Martha placed a half-pint of milk stout on the table in the snug of the Rovers. 'It lies a bit quiet for a while but doesn't bloomin' well go away.'

'What you going to do about it, Ena?'

'I've already done it. Mr Swindley's goin' to exercise the 'ouse in the mornin'.'

'Exercise, Ena? You mean flappin' your arms about and doin' knee-bends? What good'll that do?'

'Don't be so daft, Martha Longhurst.'

Martha wasn't put out. 'You've got the wrong word, Ena, and I'm goin' to ask Annie Walker. She knows nowt but long words.'

Annie Walker smiled graciously at Martha's question. 'The word is *exorcize*, not exercise. Is this Minnie Caldwell's ghost, by any chance?'

Martha nodded.

'I believe,' said Annie, 'that exorcism is best performed by the Church of England. They do follow a prescribed ritual.'

Martha's mouth dropped open. There was something different about Annie Walker these days. She was even more snobby than usual … but there was something else and it irritated Martha that she didn't know what it was.

She returned to the Snug deep in thought. 'Are your corsets too tight for you, Martha Longhurst?'

'What are you on about, Ena?'

'Your face.'

'It's *exorcize* not bloomin' PT.'

Ena shrugged. 'I'm sure that's what I said.'

'By 'eck you didn't – and you know it.'

'I'm not 'ere to argue, I'm 'ere to make sure you turn up at Minnie Caldwell's in the morning. She's twitchin' and twitterin' like an 'ungry sparrow. She'll need 'er friends.'

'Like as not I'll be there.'

Ena sighed. 'There's something on your mind, Martha. I know you too well. What's up?'

''Ave you noticed owt different about Annie Walker?'

Ena folded her arms. 'Out wi' it, Martha. She's bin botherin' you for a while so it's 'bout time you told me what's on your mind beside your usual misery.'

'I reckon Annie Walker's got an admirer.'

Ena leaned forward. 'You're like Sherlock 'Olmes you are. Who's got 'is eye on 'er, then? Whoever 'e is 'e must need his 'ead testin'.'

'Some 'ould say she was a good-lookin' woman.'

'No one round 'ere,' said Ena. 'Mind, if she didn't open her gob there might be a few blokes who'd give 'er a second glance.'

'Maybe 'e's not from round 'ere.'

Ena thought about that. 'You keep your ears open, Martha. If she is messin' with a fancy man then Jack Walker should be told.'

'Ooh, Ena, you wouldn't.'

'Wouldn't I? Jack Walker is a gent, and if she's messin' around it's my duty to warn 'im so 'e can put things right.'

'Who says it's your duty, Ena?'

Ena pulled back her shoulders and stared at Martha. 'As caretaker and resident of the Glad Tidings Mission Hall I'm specially placed to do God's work. And in the marriage vows what does it say?'

'Which bit, Ena?'

'It says, "Let no man put asunder".'

'Does it, Ena – us under what?'

'Asunder,' repeated Ena. 'Don't you know owt? Go and ask Annie "Long Words" Walker. She'll tell you. And get in another couple of milk stouts while you're at it.'

That night the siren sounded just as Annie Walker got into bed. It'll be a false alarm, she told herself. She waited for a while to see if Teresa woke up, but she didn't, and Billy and Joan both slept on. She heard low rumbles a long way away so she listened but didn't move from the warmth of her bed. If the bombing came nearer she could gather up the children and be in the cellar in less than a minute. When the all-clear sounded half an hour later she snuggled down again and had just started to drift off to sleep when she heard noises. That silly idea of Minnie Caldwell's about a ghost must be playing on my mind, she told herself. First she heard a click, then a slight thump.

'Teresa, is that you?'

There was no answer. 'Billy?' she called.

Still no answer.

When the bedroom door handle moved, Annie sat bolt upright in bed with her breath caught in her throat and her heart thumping as hard as a beer barrel on cobbles. The door opened slowly with a whining creak. Annie picked up the torch she kept on her bedside table and shone the beam at the door.

'Annie, love, it's only me,' said Jack, as he stumbled into the room.

'Jack, whyever didn't you let me know you were coming home?'

'Didn't know meself. I've only got twenty-four hours. So give us a kiss, Annie.'

Annie sensed there was something different about Jack. It was only when she did kiss him that she realized what it was. 'Jack Walker, you're drunk!'

'Correct!' he said, saluting and staggering at the same time. Annie helped him on to the bed and undressed him. 'I met some mates of mine,' he said, as she took his socks off, 'and we only 'ad a couple of pints.'

Before Annie could think of a suitable reply Jack had turned on his side and was snoring heavily. Annie lay awake miserably listening to her husband. She had never known him to be drunk before. He'd always been a gentleman, a cut above the other men in Weatherfield. Now he was like all the rest. John was a *real* gentleman. Jack had changed. She didn't know him any more and worse than that was that, just then, she didn't really care.

Minnie Caldwell hadn't slept a wink since the all-clear. She hadn't left the house because she couldn't leave her mother alone. Amy was only in her sixties but rheumatoid arthritis had crippled her and she was deaf too. The doctor had long since given up on her condition, recommending only splints and aspirin. Amy refused the splints but took the aspirin, and although Minnie found her mother hard work she loved her dearly. Amy had little appetite, and Minnie thought herself lucky that she had extra coupons and that she had an excuse for not leaving the house for every air-raid. 'I'm more than 'appy to die in me bed, Minnie,' Amy would say, 'so you get to a shelter and leave me in peace.'

When Minnie tried to argue, Amy would look up to heaven and say, 'When your number's up, it's up, and it's the Good Lord that decides, not that ruddy 'Itler.'

Minnie tossed and turned the rest of the night as every noise in the house magnified. When she heard her back door open she began to shake. She pulled the eiderdown over her ears and prayed that she was imagining things.

'It's only us,' came Ena's voice, followed

98

by heavy footsteps. Minnie looked at the clock – it was half past eight. Most days she was up by six. Hurriedly she slipped on her dressing-gown and slippers and walked downstairs, feeling so shaky she had to hold on to the bannister. 'I locked the back door,' said Minnie. ''Ow did you get in?'

'Since we know you leave the key under the flowerpot, Minnie Caldwell, it wasn't difficult,' said Ena, as she sat down. 'And, by 'eck, you look a sight – I've seen back end of a skinned pig lookin' better than you do now.'

'Leave her alone, Ena,' said Martha, straight-faced. 'You might spook 'er.'

'Go on, laugh at me,' said Minnie. 'You won't laugh when you 'ear the wailin' and the moanin'.'

'The Good Lord will see you right, Minnie,' said Ena. 'I *'ave* been prayin' for you.'

'It's done nowt to 'elp me so far.'

'I think,' said Ena, 'you should get dressed first then we should 'ave a pray 'stead of doing nowt but frettin'.'

'Yes, Ena,' said Minnie.

'Well, don't just stand there, Minnie, like Lot's wife! Get a move on.'

Minnie came down minutes later, hoping

that Ena had made a brew, but tea wasn't on Ena's mind. 'Kneel down, you two,' she said, 'we 'ave to do it right.'

The three knelt on the floor and Ena began praying: 'Dear Lord, our poor friend 'ere, Minnie Caldwell, 'as been 'avin' problems with an uneasy spirit. We know you're looking down on us but we'd be ever so grateful if–' She was interrupted by a loud knock at the front door.

Minnie gasped in surprise. 'Calm down, Minnie,' said Ena rising to her feet. 'It's not the Second Comin', it'll be Mr Swindley.'

He was a slim, dapper man whose sermons, according to Ena, 'roused as much fire in the belly as a bowl of blancmange'. But he had offered to try his hand at exorcism for a fee of half a crown, and Ena had found out that a Church of England vicar cost twice that.

Mr Swindley wandered around the room, listening at walls and muttering to himself. 'I sense there is a presence,' he said, 'but the Lord is here too.'

'Praise the Lord,' said Ena loudly.

'Yes indeed,' said Mr Swindley. 'You say the sound comes from above, Mrs Caldwell?'

Minnie looked upward fearfully. All eyes

followed hers. 'Lord,' Mr Swindley called loudly, 'Lord hear our prayer for the soul in torment. We are kneeling before you–' He broke off. 'Kneel down, everyone, close your eyes and think of the Lord.

'Lord,' he began again, 'if this poor soul has sinned in a previous life–' He broke off to clear his throat. 'And we have all sinned. She is sorry now and begs forgiveness...'

'Is it a woman?' whispered Minnie.

'That's nowt to do wi' it,' said Ena. 'Shut up and pray.'

If Mr Swindley heard, he didn't let it put him off. 'Cast her out, Lord, of this 'umble 'ome, set her free to be beside the still waters. The Lord is my shepherd, he leadeth me beside the still waters, he restoreth my soul...'

By the time they had finished the twenty-third Psalm and sung 'Guide Me O Thou Great Redeemer', their knees were aching and their throats were parched. They were all getting to their feet when they heard a thump from above.

'Hallelujah!' shouted Mr Swindley excitedly. 'The Spirit moves. Praise the Lord.'

Minnie didn't look convinced but all was silent as they listened for more noises from above.

'There,' said Mr Swindley. 'We can be sure that the good Lord's word 'as been 'eard. You'll be troubled no more. That'll be two shillings and sixpence.'

It was only an hour after everyone had left that Minnie heard weeping from above. This time she didn't put her faith in the Lord. She cried out in despair, 'Oh, Ena, what am I going to do?'

Harry Battersby and Hilda Crabtree were at the Tripe Dressers Arms and Harry had ordered the drinks. He handed Hilda hers and at first sip she thought her port and lemon tasted strange. ''Ave you put gin in this?' she asked.

He shook his head. 'Nah, don't be daft. Just sup up, 'Ilda, and be grateful.'

Hilda looked round for somewhere to deposit the drink and in the corner of the Snug noticed a wilting aspidistra. Harry began talking to the men standing at the bar and she found herself ignored. After she'd fed two drinks to the plant Harry lurched towards her. There was no doubt about it: he couldn't hold his drink and she didn't like the look in his eye.

'I'm off to powder me nose, 'Arry,' said Hilda.

''Urry back, lass. I'll be walkin' you 'ome soon.'

It sounded like a threat, and Hilda retreated to the ladies' lavatory to think through her escape plan. The back window was a bit small, even for her, and she couldn't face the indignity of getting stuck. She tidied her thick dark hair, reapplied her lipstick, pulled her shoulders back and walked out to the bar. Harry Battersby, you're not going to get the better of me, she said to herself.

He was still surrounded by a rowdy group of soldiers, but he was slumped against the bar looking as if his legs had turned to jelly. At nineteen Hilda hadn't had much experience of men but she knew that Harry no longer posed a threat. ''Arry, I'll tek you 'ome,' she said, grasping his arm.

Someone laughed. 'You be gentle with 'im lass – 'is wife'll 'it 'im with a saucepan when 'e eventually gets in.'

Hilda was shocked at this but she was too proud to show it, especially to a group of drunken men.

She half dragged Harry out of the darkness, fished in the pockets of her jacket, found her torch and shone it low on the ground. The fresh air rallied Harry and he managed to walk with only a slight list towards Hilda. 'I thought you was stayin' with yer mam,' she said. 'You should 'ave told me you was married.'

'My missus don't like me much. But you, 'Ilda, are my sort of lass.'

'That's as mebbe, 'Arry Battersby, but I'm a respectable girl and I don't go drinking with married men.'

'Does that mean,' slurred Harry, 'that I won't be seein' you again, 'Ilda?' My sweet little 'Ilda.'

'I tell yer somethin', 'Arry, if 'Itler ever rides a bike to your front door I'll 'ave a drink with yer.'

'That's a no, then, is it?'

'You're 'ome,' she said, as she propped him against his front door. 'Ta-ra.'

She'd just got to the corner of Gladstone Terrace when the siren sounded. She hesitated for a moment – which shelter? The glue-factory cellar was too smelly and she couldn't bear the warden at the Glad Tidings Mission Hall – bossy old bag. She began running down Upper Edward Street – she could run like a whippet but she'd got her best shoes on and they cramped her toes and her running style. She'd nearly made it to the Crimea Street shelter when she heard

Stukas overhead. She shone her torch upwards as if that would help her judge if one of the bombs were coming her way. 'Put that light out!' boomed a loud voice from nowhere. In her confusion she dropped her torch but carried on running until she made out the shape of the Co-op. She'd just rounded the corner when her foot hit something solid. She and one of her shoes went flying.

'What the flippin' 'eck!' The fall had winded her and the mound she'd tripped over moved. Big hands helped her to sit upright. ''Ello, chuck.' In the dark, Hilda struggled to pull down the skirt of her favourite green suit and find her shoe. 'What the 'ell are you doing sittin' there like a big dozy dog?' She didn't give him the chance to reply. 'The Stukas could come back this way. You should be in a shelter. Now, where the 'ell is me shoe? I've already lost me torch.'

'I've got mine, love.'

'Well, don't just sit there bein' gormless, 'elp me find me shoe – and don't you "love" me. My names 'Ilda Crabtree – Miss.'

'And I'm Stanley Ogden – Private 84265517.'

He took his torch from his khaki trouser

pocket and shone it in her face. She snatched it from him and shone it back in his face, but in those few seconds Stanley had seen big bright eyes and a tumble of dark hair. She looked just like his favourite aunt Cissy.

Hilda's first glimpse of Stanley surprised her. He was clean-shaven with a fine, squarish head, and as he helped her to her feet she noticed he had good strong arms. He wasn't Clark Gable but he was the nearest she'd find to him in Weatherfield. 'If you 'elp me find me shoe and me torch you can see me 'ome – if you're not too drunk.'

'I can 'old me drink,' he said. 'I just came over a bit tired like. It's me first day back in Blighty.'

'Well, it's your lucky day then, Stanley. Because if you 'adn't come over tired, like, we'd never 'ave met, would we?'

'The all-clear 'asn't sounded yet, 'Ilda.'

'Well, we'll just pretend it 'as 'cos I ain't 'oppin' on one leg to a shelter.'

'I could carry you,' said Stanley.

'Plenty of time for that, Stanley Ogden. We 'ave to get to know each other first.'

Somehow Stanley didn't doubt that Hilda Crabtree would do just that.

Now that Hilda had set her sights on Stanley Ogden she wasn't going to let him rejoin his unit without a ring on her finger.

They'd been to the pictures and Stan wanted a beer. They went into one or two pubs but didn't stay long.

'Let's go somewhere all quiet and private, like,' he'd suggested.

Hilda held tight onto his arm as they walked back to Kitchener Street. 'I know what you're after Stan. I'm doin' nowt wrong and takin' chances so you can think again.'

'I've got to be back soon 'Ilda. You might not see me again.'

'Best not to do summat I might regret, then.'

'I thought you liked me. You said I was a fine figure of a man.'

'There's nowt wrong wi' you but if I gets caught who'll look after me then?'

'If yer gets in trouble I'd 'ave to marry yer, 'Ilda.'

'Would yer, Stan?'

He shrugged. 'Yeah, why not?'

'That's settled, then.'

'What is?'

'Us getting wed.'

Stan's thoughts floundered. Eventually he

107

sorted something out. 'I meant I'd wed yer if we got caught.'

'What if I was to say, Stan, that I knew somewhere we could go tonight?' She squeezed his hand and moved closer to him. Stan smelt her *eau-de-Cologne* and was defeated.

''Ilda?'

'What?'

''Ave you been with a man before?'

She dropped his hand as if it were a hot pie. 'Stanley Ogden, 'ow dare you? I'm only nineteen and no man 'as ever as much as seen me stockin' tops.'

Stanley breathed a sigh of relief. He didn't want to admit he was still as pure as an unfired rifle. Her expectations wouldn't be that high, and he felt so excited at the mention of her stocking tops he thought getting wed was a small price to pay. After all, when the final push came in Europe he might not make it home and, if so, he would never know the pleasure of Hilda's legs with or without her stocking tops.

'All right, then, 'Ilda.'

'All right what?'

'We'll get wed. Now, where's that place we can 'ave a kiss and a cuddle?'

'When?'

'When what?'

'When can we be wed?'

'I dunno. Soon.'

'It'll 'ave to be soon 'cos you're due back. Tell you what, Stanley, we could get a special licence.'

''Ow long does that take?'

'Three days.'

Stanley had thought about it for a few minutes. It would mean going AWOL, but the thought of being alone with Hilda was overwhelming him. 'Right, then, you arrange it, 'Ilda, and we'll be wed in three days.'

She took his hand. 'Thank Gawd you've seen sense, Stanley Ogden. I'll tek you to that place I knows now.'

Stanley could hardly wait but as they walked towards the Red Rec he began to get suspicious. 'There's nowt round 'ere, 'Ilda.'

'It's not a bloomin' palace but we'll be on us own.' Hilda took Stanley's spade-like hand and, with her own torch, led him across the allotments that now took up all the spaces on the Red Rec. Each allotment owner had built his own little shed out of bits and pieces of wood and Hilda had already decided which one it was to be – her dad's. She knew where he put the key and that it was clean and tidy inside. 'This is it, then, Stan. The key's under the flower-pot.'

'Give us the torch – I can't see a ruddy thing.'

Stan lifted the flower-pot that stood to the right of the shed and stared down in the torchlight. 'There's nowt 'ere.'

'Give us that torch, Stanley. You're useless.'

Hilda shone the beam in every nook and cranny surrounding the shed. There was no key. She couldn't believe it.

'I reckon,' said Stanley, 'you've bin tryin' to lead me on. There's nowt 'ere for us. I'll tek you 'ome.'

'You'll do no such thing, Stanley Ogden. I can't abide a man who gives up easy. We'll try the other sheds – there'll be one open.'

It was wet and muddy underfoot and a light drizzle began to dampen Stanley's ardour. After finding four locked sheds he said, 'I've 'ad enough of this.'

'Shush, Stanley,' whispered Hilda. 'I can 'ear summat.'

Stanley couldn't hear a thing at first but then he caught a shuffling noise and what sounded like a woman giggling. ''Ide yerself, Stanley,' said Hilda, giving him a little push. They crouched down by the side of the shed and listened.

It was quiet for a while and Stanley's right leg went into spasm. 'I'm gettin' ruddy cramp.'

'Keep quiet,' urged Hilda. 'Give it 'ere. I'll rub it.'

Stanley tried to alter his position but sprawled across Hilda instead. A man's voice from behind them said, 'Shed's free now, mate. You two will get nowt but piles on wet ground.'

Hilda, mortified, scrabbled quickly to her feet. She heard the woman laughing but already the couple were just vague shapes in the dark.

'Did you see who it was?' she asked.

'Give over,' said Stanley, rubbing his calf muscle. 'I can't see through me arse.'

'No need for swearing, Stanley Ogden. At least now we can go inside in the dry.'

Once they were inside with the door closed there was standing room only. The shed smelt of compost and damp and Hilda hardly gave Stanley time to get his bearings. She clung round his neck, nibbling at his ears and saying, 'Oh, Stanley, we're alone at last.'

Twenty minutes later they emerged. He felt like he had when he'd got away from

Dunkirk – relieved, happy and a bit shell-shocked. Hilda had told him what to do and he'd done it. His major disappointment was that it had been too dark – he still hadn't seen her stocking tops.

'Not bad, Stanley,' said Hilda, as they made their way across the allotments. 'We'll soon be wed and then you'll learn to do it properly.'

'I've 'ad no complaints before.'

'That's as maybe, Stanley, but some girls are 'appy with owt.'

All the way back to Kitchener Street he tried to work out what she meant.

Stanley Ogden and Hilda Crabtree were married at Weatherfield Register Office by special licence. Hilda wore her green suit and a green felt hat with an added half veil. Stanley wore his Army uniform and wished he could have sunk a few pints before the ceremony. He confessed as much to Hilda. 'Never mind, Stanley,' she said. 'After we're wed we can 'ave a drink in every pub in Weatherfield.'

Stanley was grateful that the ceremony took less than ten minutes and he only felt happy after he'd had his first pint in the Tripe Dressers Arms. At each pub they went into they proclaimed they'd just got married and there was always a well-wisher to buy the next drink. Stanley felt happier and happier as the day passed.

In the evening they had a fish supper, then made their way to the Rovers.

Martha was getting in the milk stouts when they came in and she heard Stanley telling everyone he'd just got wed.

'Ena, 'ave you seen that couple at the bar?' she said, as she placed the drinks on the table.

Ena craned her neck. 'That's 'Ilda Crabtree and Stanley Ogden – they 'aven't known each other five bloomin' minutes.'

'Special licence,' said Martha. 'I 'eard them say that.'

'I think that's romantic,' said Minnie.

'You would, Minnie Caldwell,' said Ena. 'I say, "marry in 'aste repent at leisure".'

'I didn't wed in 'aste,' said Martha, 'and look what 'appened to me.'

'Your Percy 'as no stayin' power,' said Ena.

'He hasn't much with me but he managed right enough with that barmaid,' Martha said regretfully.

'Some men like trollops,' said Ena, 'and no one could accuse you of owt like that.'

Martha sighed and sipped her milk stout.

CHAPTER SEVEN

Spring 1944: Sevastopol is Liberated by the Red Army

Elsie Tanner was running out of coal, and even though it was supposed to be spring her house always seemed cold. On her way to work she'd seen women taking prams and wheelbarrows to coal collection points but she couldn't afford it anyway. Two shillings was all she had in her purse. And she was also down to her last packet of Woodbines. She'd put some wood on the fire and her last three measly lumps of coal, and watched as they smoked briefly and then went out. She took a sheet of old newspaper, held it to cover the grate, and was just about to give up when a flame burst into life. Before she could remove the newspaper it had caught fire. 'Sod and damnation!' she shouted, as she beat the life out of the paper with her brass coal shovel. Blackened bits of paper had settled on her old rug in front of the fireplace and now she needed the dustpan and brush to sweep up the mess. Now it was finally burning, the fire gave out as much heat as a bundle of matches, so she was determined not to stay in and freeze to death.

Dennis and Linda were fast asleep upstairs. It would do no harm to leave them for a couple of hours, although if she was lucky Minnie Caldwell might agree to check on them. There was a dance on at the church hall on a Wednesday evening, and although it didn't have a licence she reasoned that she and Dot might meet a couple of servicemen with money to spare for a few drinks and a bag of fish and chips.

She smoked a Woodbine from a fresh packet she'd bartered for sweet coupons and lit the oven so that the heat warmed up the scullery. Then she put on a kettle to boil so that she could have a strip wash. It was lucky she'd still got a pair of nylons left because she'd run out of gravy browning. Lots of girls her age now wore trousers but she had good legs and full hips so she had convinced herself they didn't suit her. Tonight she was going to wear a tight black skirt that came just above her knees, and a white blouse, low-cut and a bit see-through – enough, she thought, to have eyes out on stalks.

She stared in disgust at her last sliver of Lifebuoy soap and added it to the metal soap-saver with the other pieces then swished it round in the water until it went cloudy. She was just taking off her bra when she heard a commotion in the backyard and an 'Oy, you!' She lifted the kitchen blind a fraction but she couldn't see anything so she carried on washing. She'd just started towelling herself dry when the back door opened. Len Fairclough, blood streaming from his nose, staggered through the door.

They stood open-mouthed in surprise at the sight of each other. 'What the 'ell are you doin' 'ere, Len?' Before he had a chance to reply, Elsie added, 'And you can shut your gob – you've seen tits before.'

'Not like yours I 'aven't,' he said, wiping his hand across his bloody nose.

'Sit down and I'll get you cleaned up,' ordered Elsie, as she slipped into her dressing gown, then pushed Len on to a stool. 'Put your 'ead back – that'll stop it bleedin'. And then you can tell me what you're doin' 'ere.'

''Aven't you got a clean 'ankie?' he asked, as the blood dripped on to his shirt.

'You come in 'ere,' she said, as she lifted his chin back, 'bleedin' on my floor, interruptin' me wash and now you want an 'ankie?' He grinned at her and she patted his cheek. She'd met Len at Dot's wedding and they'd been to the same junior school for a short time, but any friend of Dot and Walt's was a friend of hers so she didn't feel put out.

Upstairs she found a packet of two handkerchiefs she'd had as a Christmas present. She took one out, got to the bedroom door and rushed back for the other.

It didn't take long for the bleeding to stop once she squeezed his nose for a few minutes. 'What 'appened?' she asked. 'Did you trip over me mangle?'

'Not your mangle, yer ruddy boyfriend. 'E was bendin' down puttin' somethin' on your back step and I never saw 'im in the dark. I was 'ead first in the concrete and 'e just run off. This leg of mine is a bloody nuisance.'

He pulled up his baggy grey trousers to reveal a plaster cast. 'What 'appened?' asked Elsie.

'I tripped,' said Len. 'Goin' down to the ship's boiler room. The doc says it'll take weeks to heal, mebbe months. I'm out of action for some time.'

'Some would say that were a bit of luck.'

'Not if they felt the pain,' said Len.

'So what was you doin' creepin' round my back yard?'

'I saw this strange bloke 'angin' around in the alley so I kept an eye on 'im and he came in your backyard so I followed 'im just in case 'e were up to no good.'

'Do you fancy a brew?' asked Elsie.

'Don't get me off the subject. Who is 'e, then?' asked Len, wiping the blood from his chin.

'I dunno. 'E's not me boyfriend, though – 'e just leaves me things.'

'What are yer talkin' about, Elsie?' said Len sharply. 'I 'ope you're not doin' owt stupid.'

'It's none of your business, Len Fair-clough, so don't take that tone with me.'

Len said quietly, 'I want us to be mates, and I don't see why you've got strange blokes leaving things on your back step.'

Elsie stiffened. 'If you must know, Dot and I put little notes in the RAF uniforms with our addresses and I've been left little presents.'

'What about Dot? Is 'e leavin' little presents for 'er too?'

'Nowt I know of.'

'Don't you think that's strange – that 'e picked on you.'

''Appen I didn't think about it.'

''Appen you should, then.'

'What are you getting' at, Len? There's no 'arm. I haven't even met 'im. I 'ardly know you, so mind yer own...'

He was staring at her. 'Just you think on, Elsie. I'm staying around 'ere for a while. Vi's puttin' me up at the moment and Dot said I should keep an eye out for you–'

'She's got a bloody nerve!' interrupted Elsie. 'I don't need the likes of you, Len Fairclough, breathin' down me neck and you can tell 'er that from me.' She resolved to tell Dot exactly what she thought of her interference.

Len made no move to leave and Elsie's impatience grew. 'There's that saying,' said Len, '"Beware of Greeks bearing gifts".'

'Was 'e a Greek?'

''Ow the 'ell could I tell?'

'Was 'e tall?'

''Appen 'e was.'

'And you didn't see 'is face?'

'Your yard is as black as a coal-'ole. I couldn't see me 'and in front of me.'

Elsie took a close look at Len's nose. 'It looks a bit swollen but it's stopped bleedin',' she said. 'You can go back to Dot and tell 'er to get round 'ere. I want words with 'er.'

'What about me tea?' asked Len.

'Get Dot to make you a brew.'

Len limped out to the backyard and before he'd opened the back gate Elsie had retrieved the package. She couldn't wait to open it. When she did she couldn't believe her luck: Player's cigarettes – hundreds of them. She didn't hear Len's return.

'Couldn't wait, could you?' said Len from the open back door. 'You just smoke your ruddy fags. But don't think they're for nowt. 'E'll be back. 'E's after yer body.'

''Ere, catch!' she called, throwing a packet towards him. 'And you listen to me, Len Fairclough. I admit my body's been 'ad a few times, me 'usband being the worst cos 'e left me reminders. But I'll tell you this much – I'd 'ave enjoyed meself a ruddy sight more if I'd 'ad presents like this bloke leaves.'

'You know what you are?' yelled Len. 'Nowt but a tart!'

'Get out, Len,' Elsie shrieked, 'and bloody well don't come back! Think on this – there's worse things than being a tart. At least I gets pleasure, which is a ruddy sight more than I ever got with my Arnold.'

'I'm off,' said Len. 'You're as stubborn as a ruddy mule. You need a man to take you in 'and. You've got no coal, the 'ouse is bloody freezin' and all you want to do is get yer knickers down for a few fags.'

Elsie picked up the frying-pan and clenched her fist. 'Just mind your own business and sod off, Len, or you'll be 'avin' another bloody nose.'

As a final gesture Len threw the cigarettes back into the kitchen then slammed the door.

Elsie sighed as she picked up the packet, opened it and lit a cigarette. She inhaled deeply. After two drags she felt calmer. This is me, she thought. I'm not going to smoke Woodbines for ever more. I'm a Player's girl now.

Next time she'd be waiting for her mystery man because, whoever he was, he was a good provider. And that was more than could be said for a few men she'd been in the sack with, Steve Tanner being the only exception. He'd been in a different league altogether.

An hour later Dot peered round the kitchen door, looking sheepish. 'Do I need a white flag or shall I wave me knickers in the air?'

Elsie tried not to smile. 'What makes you think I need the likes of Len Fairclough keeping an eye on me?'

'Elsie, you've no 'usband worth speakin' of, no dad, no brother and no boyfriend. You need someone to rely on.'

'I rely on myself, Dot Greenhalgh, and don't you forget it.'

'I see you've got some fags,' Dot observed.

'Yeah, but if you say owt else to Len I'll stop sharin' with you.'

On their way to Minnie Caldwell, who was always soft enough to say she'd look in on the kids, Elsie said, 'Anyway, Len with a peg-leg wouldn't be much 'elp to me.'

'Don't take the mick, Elsie. According to a letter I've 'ad from Walt, Len was a real 'ero. Did 'e tell you he slipped?'

Elsie nodded.

'Well, he slipped 'cos their ship was bombed and his leg got smashed, but he teks no notice of the fact 'is bones is pokin' through his bell bottoms and manages to haul three blokes up from the flooded boiler room. And if 'e doesn't get a medal 'e bloody well should.'

'I've always thought he was a good bloke,' said Elsie, ashamed of herself. 'But I still don't need 'im to spy on me.'

At home in Jubilee Terrace Minnie Caldwell

was a disappointed woman. Her mother wouldn't settle and the noises were worse than ever. Even more worryingly, half a pork pie and half a loaf of bread had gone missing from the pantry. And it wasn't the first time food had gone missing. At first she thought it was just her memory going and she'd eaten it herself. But now she knew. Someone had been in her house. She'd never ever locked the back door, there had been no need, and since she'd lost the key she couldn't lock it now. It was probably a hungry tinker, she thought, and she hoped he had needed that pork pie and bread more than she did. She'd only had a slice of bread and marge with treacle for her tea but since the noises had started she'd lost her appetite.

She'd just put some soda in her washing-up water when a knock came at the back door. She jumped in surprise and the box flew out of her hand, soda crystals spreading all over the scullery floor. 'By 'eck!' she muttered as she opened the door. 'Oh, it's you. You can come in.'

All dressed up, Elsie entered, followed by Dot. 'Did we startle you?' asked Elsie. Minnie didn't answer, she just got down on her knees and began scooping up the crystals. Elsie and Dot joined in. 'What's up, Mrs Caldwell?' asked Elsie, seeing that she looked close to tears and wasn't her usual self at all.

Minnie told her about her ghost, the nightly noises and the visit from Mr Swindley. She also told them about the missing pork pie, and finally admitted that other food had been taken.

'Ghosts don't need food,' said Elsie. ''Ave you looked in yer loft?'

'The openin's too small for a body to get through.'

'Let's 'ave a look anyway,' suggested Elsie – the sooner Minnie was sorted out the more likely it was she'd look in on the kids.

They trooped upstairs to look at the twelve by twelve inches of the loft hatch.

'It's not likely to be a German parachutist,' said Elsie. 'They eat too much to be that small.'

'German prisoner-of-war?' suggested Dot.

Elsie shook her head. 'They get better fed than we do.'

Minnie said, in a whisper, 'We ain't never goin' to find out, are we?'

'Aye, we will, so don't you fret,' said Elsie.

'My mam's got a ladder,' said Dot, 'and Len Fairclough's staying and 'is 'ead ain't twelve inches square so at least 'e can 'ave a look.'

'What about Ena?' asked Minnie.

'What about 'er?'

'She'll want to be 'ere. She'll think I've gone behind 'er back.'

'Is she in Rovers?'

'Aye, more than likely,' said Minnie rue-fully.

'You get round there and get her, then,' Elsie said, giving Minnie an encouraging push. 'Dot, I've got nowt to say to Len, so you go round and ask 'im to bring 'is little ladder.'

'We'll never get to the dance at this rate,' said Dot, looking disappointed.

'The blokes 'ardly mek a move till last dance,' said Elsie, 'so we'll still manage that and a fish supper if we're lucky.'

Once they'd gone Elsie sat on the floor and listened. A few minutes later she heard a scrabbling noise. 'Oh, my Gawd!' she said aloud, as the thought sprang into her mind that it might be rats.

Ena Sharples, Minnie and Martha turned up seconds before Len and his ladder. With six people on the tiny landing it was shoulder to shoulder and Len had to raise his voice. 'Come on, you lot, stop mitherin' and move out me way.' There was some shuffling about. 'Well, get on wi' it, lad,' said Ena, peeved at the idea of Elsie Tanner taking the initiative. 'We've got milk stouts waitin' on us at Rovers.'

With the ladder in position Elsie murmured to Len, 'Are you sure you can do this with your leg? I can go up there as long as I tek me shoes off.'

'You just 'old the ladder, Elsie. I'll be slow but I'll do it.'

Len inched up the ladder, dragging his plastered leg behind him. Eventually he made it to the loft hatch. 'I can't see 'owt,' he said. 'I'll need a torch.'

'Minnie Caldwell – torch!'

At Ena's command Minnie rushed downstairs. Martha stood silent, her face set in its usual sombre expression. Dot giggled nervously and Elsie hoped the whole episode would soon be over and she'd either be dancing or in the pub with some nice-looking bloke with money in his pocket.

Once Len had the torch they waited for his verdict, staring upwards in silence. 'There's nowt I can see,' he said, 'but there's an 'orrible smell.' He carried on scanning with his torch for some time until Ena grew irritable. 'Good thing you're not an ack-ack man, Len Fairclough,' she said. "Ow long is it goin' to take you to realize there's nothing up there?'

'You're wrong, Mrs Sharples. There *is* something up 'ere.'

That shut Ena up and again they waited.

'Come out, whoever you are,' Len shouted. Then there was a sound they couldn't fail to recognize: someone was sobbing. 'We won't 'urt you. Come on – show yerself.'

After a few moments Len gasped. 'Ye gods!'

'What is it?' they all shouted at once.

'It's a little lad, an' 'e's in a bad way.'

"Ow could 'e get up there?' asked Minnie, amazed.

"E 'ad 'elp, of course,' said Ena. 'Come on then, Len, tell 'im to come down.'

'Come on, lad,' said Len gently. 'You need 'elp. Come towards me. Don't be scared.'

He switched off the torch. 'I'll go back down,' he called into the dark of the loft, 'and you 'ave a little think.'

Len came down the ladder painfully slowly, his face grim. 'He's scared to death. I don't think he's goin' to budge. Got any ideas?'

It was Ena who spoke first. 'He might

come out for another little 'un.'

'Who do you suggest, Mrs Sharples?' said Len. 'A bloomin' tooth fairy?'

'There's no need for cheek,' said Ena sharply. 'What about Kenneth Barlow? 'E's a bright lad, and not an 'aporth of fat on 'im.'

'He'll be asleep in bed. Ida won't like it.'

'Don't argue with me, Len Fairclough. That lad's in and out of 'is bed like a yo-yo during the raids. She'll let 'im come if you ask 'er proper.'

Len went off immediately. Now that the loft was open they could clearly hear the boy's quiet sobbing. 'I can't stand 'ere doin' nowt,' said Elsie. 'I'm goin' up. Dot, you 'old the ladder for me.' For once Ena kept quiet. No one was going to see *her* bloomers.

Elsie shone the torch on what she thought at first was a pile of old rags, until they moved and a little head raised itself. Eyes half closed, he squinted at the beam of light then his head sank down again. 'It's all right, pet. You can come down. Honest.' There was no response.

Ten minutes later Kenneth Barlow turned up holding Len's hand. He wore a coat over blue-striped pyjamas and wellington boots.

He looked a little scared and still had a crease mark of sleep on his face.

'Will you be all right on the ladder, son?' Len asked.

'I think so,' said Kenneth solemnly, as he slipped off his coat.

'I'll be right behind you,' said Len, 'so you've got no worries. Once you're through I'll 'and you the torch.'

Kenneth went up without looking down and easily squeezed through into the loft space. They could hear him talking but not the response. After some time Kenneth's face appeared. 'He thinks you're Nazis and you'll take him back.'

'Back where?' asked Len.

'To a place where they were cruel to 'im.'

'You tell 'im,' shouted Ena before Len could reply, 'that we'll look after 'im.'

'I'll 'ave to pull him along,' said Kenneth. ''E says 'e can't stand.'

'Do your best, Kenneth, lad,' urged Len.

Shortly afterwards they heard thumping noises and whimpering, and then eventually Kenneth's wellies appeared. Len moved down the ladder two rungs as Kenneth emerged. Finally they saw the face of their 'ghost' – a little white face, eyes half closed with yellow pus, hair matted. 'Come down

129

backward, lad, like Kenneth,' Len encouraged him. 'You just look up, not down.'

Kenneth smiled broadly as his feet reached the floor. 'You're a little 'ero,' said Minnie, and gave him a hug. By now Len had grabbed the boy to stop him falling from the last two rungs. He scooped him up in his arms and stared down into the ashen face. The lad was soaking wet, filthy, and weighed no more than a bundle of sticks.

'Don't just stand there, Len Fairclough!' yelled Ena. 'Get that baby downstairs by the fire.'

'The sergeant major's in charge now,' whispered Elsie to Dot, as they followed Len to the back room.

'What was that, Elsie Tanner?'

'Just sayin' you'll know what to do, Mrs Sharples.'

''Appen we'll all 'ave to do our bit.'

Len watched the boy's face worriedly. ''E's in a reet bad way, Mrs Sharples.'

'Nowt that a bit o' warmth, a sup of tea and some food won't put right,' she replied. 'Minnie, fetch blankets and towels. Elsie, put the kettle on. Dot, get the tin bath down from 'ook.'

'No orders for me, Mrs Sharples?' asked Len.

Ena fixed him with her most withering look. 'You take young Kenneth 'ome, and tell Ida he did a champion job.' She patted Kenneth on the head, slipped sixpence into his hand, then held out her arms. 'Pass the baby over, Len, and tell no one about this. Kenneth, you don't want to end up in 'ell do you?'

'No, Mrs Sharples.'

'Well, say nowt except to your mam and tell her to say nowt to anyone. I'll be in to see 'er in the morning.'

It took some time to half fill the tin bath with hot water. It was placed in front of the fire and Ena gently undressed the child when everything was ready to her satisfaction.

''E stinks something awful,' said Dot.

'So would you,' said Ena 'if you'd been in a loft for weeks.'

Minnie had brewed tea and made a bowl of bread and milk for the boy. 'Put plenty of sugar on it, Minnie – and, you two, off you go.'

Elsie and Dot needed no second telling, but as they got to the back door Ena shouted, 'Elsie Tanner, if you've left those kids of yours alone, think on this baby and get yourselves off 'ome.'

'Mitherin' old bag,' muttered Elsie, knowing their night out was ruined. Neither of them could forget that pathetic little scrap. 'Mebbe I should go 'ome,' she said then, uncertainly.

'Aye,' said Dot. 'I'm not in the mood for dancing either. I'll come with you.'

'How's your Sally's baby?' asked Elsie.

Dot smiled. 'Our Clark's grand. Sally's still a bit tired but me mam 'elps 'er ever such a lot.'

'I wish I 'ad a mam to 'elp me,' said Elsie, as she linked arms with Dot. They both shivered in the frosty night air and hurried along, their breath visible in the dark.

In the back alley Elsie said, 'Do you fancy a fish supper?'

'I fancy some chips.'

'Right, then,' said Elsie, 'chips it is,' and they set off for the fish shop.

CHAPTER EIGHT

Spring 1944: U-515 and U-68 Sunk by US

Now that Annie had help with Billy and Joan she had a little more time to herself. The Rovers closed at two o'clock on Sundays and didn't open again until seven. Annie had found John Barnstable the ideal companion for Sunday afternoons. Their only problem was finding somewhere to go that was well away from Weatherfield. Occasionally John borrowed a friend's Ford motor car and brought a picnic tea. Then he drove to the Peaks and they ate their sandwiches and drank a flask of tea. Sometimes, if it wasn't too cold or wet, they walked. Annie found that she didn't mind a bit when John held her hand.

Teresa had Mondays off and an evening in the week. She went to early Mass on Sunday morning and afterwards spent time with Billy reading him Aesop's fables or Bible stories. Annie's only concern was that she had found Billy once with rosary beads, but she consoled herself with the thought that he was much better behaved now.

Occasionally Teresa asked awkward questions. 'Where will you be off to today, then, Mrs Walker?'

'I'm seeing my friends in Manchester again.'

'You've been visiting them a lot lately,' Teresa said, as she bent down to pick up Joan.

Annie didn't like the expression on the girl's face. It was as if the little madam *knew*.

'They *are* very good friends,' said Annie.

'You're lucky, Mrs Walker. I don't have any friends.'

Annie wasn't surprised: there was something a little too pious about the girl but at least she didn't drop her Hs like most people in Weatherfield.

'I'll be back for opening time,' said Annie. 'If there's a raid you know what to do.'

'Of course, Mrs Walker.'

Outside it was drizzling and the sky was grey. Annie pulled up her fur collar and walked briskly to Bessie Street School. It was risky meeting John there but she reasoned that if anyone saw them she would say that he had offered her a lift to her friends in Manchester.

As she sat beside him in the car Annie realized that part of her excitement stemmed from their meetings being so clandestine. She truly liked John but her heart was Jack's. Even so, when she hadn't seen Jack for months and months she could hardly remember his face. His last unexpected leave had been short and miserable. He'd been hung over the next morning and had spent most of the day in bed. He'd been morose and had taken little interest in the Rovers or the children and he had ignored Teresa. He wasn't the Jack she had known of old. Occasionally she wondered if she was keeping John in reserve in case Jack didn't come back at all. Every week she heard of some poor woman who'd had the dreaded telegram. John Barnstable was her war insurance policy.

'You're looking lovely, Annie,' he said now, as he patted her gloved hand.

To Annie compliments were like the cream on strawberries – delicious and essential. John made her feel young and desirable, even though they had only kissed and held hands. For Annie that was enough.

As he drove through empty streets and out towards the Peaks, the rain turned to sleet but they barely noticed. Once they were into open country John stopped the car and they ate salmon sandwiches, a real treat, and talked about their week. They hardly noticed when the sleet turned to snow.

'We'd best be getting nearer town before it gets dark,' said John. Annie felt disappointed the time had slipped by so quickly. She was happy just to be away from the Rovers for a few hours, and she felt quite intoxicated by the hand-holding and kissing.

He started the drive back under darkening skies. Dense grey clouds gathered ominously and driving snow beat against the windscreen. A few miles on, the snow became a blizzard. John stopped the car in a country lane. 'We can't go on,' he said, 'until this clears somewhat.'

By now it was five o'clock and dark. Annie shivered and he put an arm around her. 'We'll just have to snuggle up,' he said, as he gave her a playful squeeze. Annie giggled. There was plenty of time to get back to the Rovers.

Ena Sharples stood outside the Rovers in the snow at just after seven and was shocked to find the door locked. The pub had once run out of beer but she'd never known it not open on time. Soon a few others joined her, Albert Tatlock and Tom Hewitt from No. 7, and finally Martha Longhurst. 'Well,' said Ena, 'we'll achieve nowt standin' 'ere stampin' our feet and gettin' frostbite. I'm goin' round the back.'

'She keeps it locked, Mrs Sharples,' said Albert.

Ena glowered at him as though he were responsible somehow. 'There's that lass who's got "nun" written all over 'er face – she'll unlock it.'

'If there's anyone there at all, Ena,' said Martha. 'It seems reet quiet and deserted to me.'

'Martha, this isn't the *Marie Celeste,* this is the bloomin' Rovers.

'Aye. But it seems a bit strange, don't it?'

Ena thought it seemed very strange indeed, but she wasn't going to admit it. 'I'm goin' round the back. You lot please yerselves.'

Eventually Teresa answered the back door. 'What kept yer?' asked Ena.

'Mrs Walker told me not to open the back door to anyone.'

'And where might Mrs Walker be at this moment?'

'She's visiting her friends in Manchester.'

'Didn't know she 'ad any friends.'

'She often sees them on Sunday afternoons.'

'That's as mebbe but she'll want the Rovers to be tekkin' brass so stand aside and let me through.'

Behind the pebble glasses Teresa's eyes widened. 'Oh, I couldn't let you in. Mrs Walker would never forgive me.'

'She'll never forgive losin' good beer money, so you can let me pass.'

'Jesus, Mary and Joseph,' murmured Teresa.

'Did Jesus turn water into wine, lass?' asked Ena.

She nodded. 'Well, think on me as God's right 'and at the Mission. 'E's called on me to turn water into wine.'

Teresa thought about that for a moment. 'But that was at a wedding.'

'And this is wartime, girl. Out of my way.'

Teresa shrank back as Ena Sharples barged past. Then she crossed herself for luck and ran upstairs to guard her charges.

Once the door was opened Ena designated Albert Tatlock barman and Tom Hewitt cellarman. They didn't argue, and soon Albert was taking orders and working the pumps as if he'd been doing it all his life.

'It's funny Ned ain't 'ere either,' said Martha. 'You don't think Annie Walker's with 'im, do you, Ena?'

'Sometimes, Martha Longhurst, you amaze me.'

'Why's that, Ena?'

'Because you're such a blitherin' idiot. Annie Walker may be a lot of things but she's not blind, deaf or daft. If she'd've 'ad a choice between 'Immler or Ned Narkin, she'd 'ave chosen 'Immler.'

Martha pursed her lips. Maybe Ned Narkin was a long shot but Annie Walker *was* seeing a man, of that she remained sure. And one day she'd find out who it was, just so that she could tell Ena Sharples and see her surprised. For once Martha would be first in line with a bit of news.

Time went by and there was still no sign of Annie Walker. More people came in, stood at the bar and waited while Albert Tatlock used the pumps with slow deliberation. Hilda Ogden walked in and pretty soon was announcing in a loud voice at the bar, 'I'm tellin' yer what I saw and it's God's 'onest truth. I *did* see Mrs Walker in a car with a man. They looked … friendly, if you knows what I mean.'

In seconds Ena was behind her. 'I've 'eard

of you, 'Ilda Ogden. There's nothin' you like better than a bit o' gossip but don't you come in 'ere spreadin' lies and causin' trouble.'

Hilda bridled. 'I don't 'ave to stay 'ere to be insulted.'

'That's true,' said Ena. 'You could be insulted anywhere.'

Hilda stuck her chin in the air. 'I wouldn't 'ave another drink in 'ere if it was the last pub in the world,' she said, and with a clatter of high heels she left the Rovers.

When Ena had sat down in the snug, Martha said, 'I thought you didn't even like Annie Walker and there you are standin' up for 'er like a good 'un.'

'I don't like 'er, Martha Longhurst, but I'll be blowed if I lets a little madam like 'Ilda Ogden start gossip mongerin'.'

'Want to do it yerself, do you, Ena?'

Ena frowned. 'There's nowt wrong wi' Annie Walker as a landlady. She keeps this place better than most.'

'Didn't I tell you she was carryin' on with someone? Didn't I tell yer first but yer didn't believe me?'

When in doubt Ena ignored what didn't suit her. 'Sup up, Martha. Let's get round to Minnie and see 'ow the little lad's doin.'

"E's said nowt and 'e's bin with Minnie for days.'

'Aye,' said Ena. 'Minnie's the right one to care for 'im, though. 'E's come on gradely since she's bin feedin' 'im. 'E'll talk in 'is own time.'

'Where's 'e come from, though, Ena? They'll want 'im back.'

Ena fixed her friend with a steely look. 'That lad will go nowhere but where 'e wants. I'm tellin' you that now so don't you forget it. I like kids and I 'ate those that are cruel to 'em.'

'What about the authorities? They'll come after 'im.'

'We'll 'ide 'im. The whole bloomin' street will 'ide 'im. Do you 'ear me?'

'Minnie can't keep 'im for ever,' said Martha, adjusting her beret. 'What about 'is ration books? What about 'is schooling.'

Ena shrugged. 'Ada Hayes is a teacher. She'll know what to do.'

They were just putting on their coats when the siren wailed, and soon they could see smoke rising over Manchester.

'Good thing there's no full moon tonight,' said Ena. 'There's nowt I 'ate more than them Stinkers.'

Martha walked on, nodding in agreement.

She hated them too. On the night of a full moon, drums of oil were moved into the middle of certain streets in Weatherfield and one of the ARP came round and lit them. Great black clouds of smoke rose up and no one could see a hand in front of them. 'It's me winders and me blinds I 'ate cleaning the next day,' said Martha, 'and I've 'eard some parts of the country don't bother.'

'That's 'cos they've got better shelters than us,' said Ena, as they approached Minnie's house. 'Now, stop mitherin' and lets get on wi' it.'

When the siren sounded Minnie Caldwell had placed pillows and blankets under her heavy table. Amy had said, 'Leave me be – it won't be owt,' so Minnie had made a brew and helped her mother drink it from an invalid's cup.

Since he'd been staying with her the boy hadn't spoken to her, but he had spoken to Amy and Mabel, the cat, although Minnie knew he spoke too quietly for her mother to hear. She'd found out this evening that his name was Dieter Holliman. He'd refused to go to bed upstairs and she'd made him up a bed between two armchairs near the fire. His arms and legs were matchstick thin and the bedrooms were unheated so Minnie had been glad to keep him by the warmth of the fire.

Just before the siren had sounded Minnie was in the scullery and he'd been stroking the cat on his lap. 'Your name is Mabel,' he'd said, in his precise way, 'and I am Dieter Holliman.' Minnie noticed he had an accent but she didn't know what it was. His name could have been German but she didn't care – he was such a poor little scrap. However, even in the short time he had been with her Minnie had seen great improvements. She'd bathed his eyes every hour with boiled warm water and a pinch of salt for two days and now they were clear. Even his cheeks seemed plumper. She noticed that he tried to hide food under cushions or in his pockets so she gave him extra, saying, 'You save that for later, pet.' And when he smiled for the first time, Minnie was so pleased she thought she'd burst.

The sirens worried him but not so much as someone knocking on the door. It was then that he trembled in fear.

'Come on, Dieter, you snuggle down with me under the table,' said Minnie. 'Bring Mabel with you.'

Minnie was so tired that she fell asleep and slept through the raid and the all-clear.

Ena's voice woke her, though. 'Minnie Caldwell, the street could be reduced to bloomin' ashes and you wouldn't know a thing about it.'

Minnie crawled out from under the table as Ena and Martha stared down at her. 'Ooh, it 'asn't 'as it, Ena?'

'No, Minnie – yer daft bat – it's still standin'. Manchester got a right 'ammerin', though.'

'Poor souls,' murmured Minnie.

'How's your other poor soul?' Ena asked, pointing towards the sleeping boy.

'He's champion, Ena. Good as gold 'e's been. He spoke to Mabel tonight. He says 'is name is Dieter Holliman.'

'Sounds foreign like.'

'I think 'e's German,' said Minnie.

''E looks German,' agreed Martha.

'Who asked you, Martha Longhurst? What do you mean, 'e looks German? I don't think 'e looks a bit like 'Itler or 'Immler or Goering.'

'Aren't Germans supposed to 'ave fair 'air and blue eyes?'

'Them three I've just mentioned 'aven't.'

Peeved, Martha sat down and folded her

arms. 'You just 'ave to be *right* about every blessed thing.'

Ena smiled. 'That's because I'm not wrong 'bout most things. Now, Minnie, you put kettle on. We 'ave things to talk about.'

'What sort of things, Ena?'

'For one, what are we going to do about little lad, and two, 'ow do we keep Annie Walker on the straight and narrer?'

'What do yer mean, Ena?'

'You mek a brew, Minnie, and I'll tell yer.'

CHAPTER NINE

Spring 1944: No Civilian Casualties in May

Elsie Tanner stopped at the fish and chip shop on her way home from work. It hadn't been a good day: her machine had gone wrong three times and Dot hadn't been there to have a laugh with – she had the flu. There was a long, slow-moving queue, her feet ached and her admirer hadn't left her a gift since Len Fairclough had fallen over him in the dark.

'What'll it be, Elsie?' asked Joe Jackson, the fish-shop owner. Joe had a big, round, permanently red face and he wrapped his fare faster than the eye could follow.

'Roe and chips, please, Joe.'

'Cheer up, it might never 'appen,' he said, giving her a wink, which meant he'd given her extra for the kids. 'When are yer comin' dancin' with me, darlin'?'

Elsie forced a smile. 'When yer wife gives me permission.'

He shrugged and wiped the sweat from his

forehead. 'You go careful, Elsie – you're one of me best customers.'

She was tempted to eat a few chips on the way home but it was raining so she walked as fast as she could, holding the warm package in her hands. She was soaked by the time she got home. The house was in darkness and just for a moment she'd forgotten where she'd left her kids. She was turning on the gas lamps when she remembered – a girl in Gas Street had them, a sister of Amy Clutterbuck who worked at the factory. She'd promised to walk them back at seven. It was ten to now.

She ate her roe and a few chips, then read the newspaper they were wrapped in. The news had been mainly good lately – but if it was that good, she thought, why wasn't the war over yet? Allied bombers had destroyed Cassino in Italy. She wondered if Steve had been sent out there – she hoped so: she'd heard Italy was a warm country. 'Not like this freezing 'ole,' she said aloud.

Once the fire was lit and roaring, she took off her coat. Then she put the rest of the chips in a low oven and sat down to smoke one of her last Player's cigarettes.

Minutes later Amy Clutterbuck's sister arrived, a sour-faced woman in her thirties.

'Your Dennis 'as got a scurvy 'ead, sticky eyes and his bum's sore,' she said, as she propped him, still asleep, in an armchair.

Elsie shrugged. 'Our Dennis, 'as always got somethin'. What about Linda?'

'She wet herself twice.' Linda hung her head and ran to her mother.

'She's scared of the outside privy. Someone 'as to go wi' 'er.'

'That's as maybe, Mrs Tanner, but she's too old to wet 'erself.'

'I'll tell 'er that. 'Ow much do I owe you?'

'That'll be two and six.'

'Aye.' Elsie rooted in her purse. 'I've only got two bob. I'll 'ave to give you the other sixpence tomorrow. I'll give it to your sister.'

When Frozen Face had gone Elsie muttered, 'I'll 'ave to borrow it from your sister first.'

'Mam,' said Linda, pulling at her skirt, 'I don't like 'er. She's like a witch.'

'You won't 'ave to go there again, pet. I'll find someone better.'

'You always say that, Mam.'

'It's the war, our Linda. Would yer like some chips and a cuppa?'

Linda put her arms round Elsie's neck. 'I think you're the best mam in the world.'

'What you anglin' for?'

'Can I sleep in your bed, Mam?'

'Aye. If you promise not to wet it.'

Linda pushed her little face towards Elsie and kissed her cheek. 'Mam?'

'What?'

'That Mrs Clatter said you was a tart. What's she mean?'

Elsie might have felt insulted if anyone else had said it but the woman did have a prize face – ugly as a box of frogs. 'It means, our Linda, that the old bag doesn't like men and they don't like 'er.'

The explanation was beyond Linda. 'Can I 'ave me chips now, Mam?'

Later, with both children asleep in her bed, Elsie did some washing and listened to Glenn Miller on the wireless. She felt bored to tears and was planning to go to bed early. She'd just stripped to her underwear for a wash by the fire when there was a knock at the back door.

'Come on in, then,' she called out, glad to have a visitor. 'I've nowt on so if you're a fella close yer eyes.' It was a joke, of course. She thought it might be Dot having dragged herself out of her sick bed or Sally wanting a break from baby Clark. She didn't expect a complete stranger holding a bottle of whisky and a bunch of flowers. 'Oh, Gawd,' she said, grabbing her cardigan and covering herself.

'Bella! Bella!' he said.

He was tall with thick black hair and dark brown eyes. He was also the best-looking man she'd ever seen in Weatherfield. And she'd always preferred the RAF blue. 'No, I'm not Bella,' she managed to say. 'I'm Elsie.'

He smiled, showing perfect white teeth. '*Bella* means beautiful and you are.'

'You're not from round 'ere, are you?'

He shook his head. 'Born in Manchester – my dad was Italian – Antonio Bartolini at your service.' He bent to take her hand, lifted it to his mouth and kissed it slowly. Then he looked deep into her eyes and Elsie was lost. She guessed that Antonio Bartolini could teach her a thing or two, especially after she'd had a whisky or three.

Antonio didn't rush. He poured the drinks, sat opposite her and told her about his family's ice cream business and how he'd been interned on the Isle of Man for a few weeks. When he'd been given clearance he'd joined the RAF and now he was a flying instructor. He'd found her note and liked the sound of her. 'And now I've met you, Elsie. And I mean it when I say you're like a goddess.'

Elsie had never met such a man before. His voice was as deep and warm as a hot toddy and he had class. Steve had been classy, too, but even he didn't quite have Antonio's easy charm. And when Antonio kissed her he didn't ram his tongue straight down her throat like some men, he nibbled a little at her lips then whispered in her ear that she was not only the most beautiful woman he'd ever met but the most exciting. Elsie was old enough to know better but she still liked to hear such things.

They'd drunk two whiskies and Elsie was beginning to regret letting the kids sleep in her bed. Antonio was showing her how to dance the tango when a little voice at the door said, 'Mam, Dennis is cryin'.'

Elsie sighed with disappointment, but Antonio smiled broadly at the little girl. 'Hello,' he said, taking her hand and kissing it. 'You're as beautiful as your mother.' Linda giggled.

'I'll go up to 'im,' said Elsie. 'Come on, Linda, back to bed.'

'Leave her for a while,' said Antonio. 'I like *bambini*. Let's see what I have in my coat pocket for a pretty girl.'

Linda's pudgy hands clutched at the bar of

chocolate he produced and she'd torn the paper off in seconds. 'And some Du Maurier for the lady,' he said, laying four packets on the table.

Dennis settled quickly enough with a nappy change and his dummy, and when Elsie came downstairs Linda was sitting on Antonio's lap with her face covered in chocolate. 'Gerroff, pet,' said Elsie irritably. 'You'll get chocolate on 'is lovely uniform.'

'It's all right. I've got to go now, anyway,' Antonio said.

Elsie couldn't contain herself. 'Don't go yet. Linda's off to bed after I've washed her face.'

Antonio kissed the top of Linda's head and put her on the floor. She'd eaten all the chocolate and was now licking her fingers. 'I have to be back at the base, Elsie. I'm flying tomorrow.'

As he was leaving, the thought crossed Elsie's mind that maybe she wouldn't see him again. Her kids put off a lot of men. But then he kissed her hard and gently squeezed her left breast, murmuring in her ear, 'I'll take you dancing tomorrow night.'

'Aye. If yer like,' she answered trying to sound nonchalant.

She washed Linda's face and laid her

alongside Dennis in the double bed. Then she came downstairs and poured herself a whisky. She picked up a packet of Du Maurier and held it for a moment. Du Maurier was a lady's fag. They didn't taste as good as Player's but, like Antonio, they had class. It was then that she noticed the folded slip of paper. It read – 'Elsie, make me a happy man and buy yourself something nice with this.'

Elsie picked up the crisp white five-pound notes. A tenner! With a tenner she could do so much. A little voice in her head said, 'You can't take that.' But a louder voice said, 'With that much money you could take a few days off work and still buy something.'

'Sod it,' she said aloud. 'I'm 'avin' it.' She smiled to herself – 'avin' it in more ways than one, but at least this time the man knew how to treat a woman and he looked like a film star. She'd given others her all for nowt, so why not enjoy herself now?

Ida Barlow and Bessie Tatlock had spent the evening surrounded by old clothes. A few other women had shown interest in a make-do-and-mend group but no one had turned up. 'Folks round 'ere are always slow to catch on to summat new,' said Bessie. 'We'll just 'ave to do what we can with our old stuff.' So they unpicked seams and Ida sketched a few ideas on brown paper.

''Ow's Minnie Caldwell gettin' on wi' little lad?' asked Bessie.

'Our Kenneth's been round to see 'im. They seem to be getting along like an 'ouse on fire.'

'Your Kenneth needs a little mate.'

Ida nodded ''E seems 'appier since 'e's met him.'

'It's a wonder Minnie Caldwell can afford to feed a young lad.'

'She can't,' said Ida, as she sucked the end of her pencil. 'I've been sendin' 'er a few rock cakes and some scones. Minnie says he's so 'ungry he'd "eat a scabby 'oss between two slices o' bread".'

Bessie laughed. 'I've got some bottled fruit and pickled eggs that'll 'elp 'er out, but she can't keep 'im forever, can she?'

'Kenneth said 'im and two older boys ran away from an orphanage in Manchester. The lad's Jewish.'

'Poor little mite,' said Bessie. 'If 'alf what we've bin 'earin' about is true I bet 'e 'asn't got a soul left.'

Ida put down her pencil and gazed at her designs. 'Kenneth said 'e escaped from

Germany before the war with 'is mam, but you know what kids are like – full of daft stories.'

Bessie nodded. 'Let's 'ave a look at yer drawings, then.' She picked up the sheet of brown paper and studied it carefully. 'By 'eck, Ida, you are a clever girl. If you colour 'em in with some of Kenneth's crayons I reckon we're in business. A few bob 'ere and there would 'elp you out.'

Ida nodded, but what was more important to her was the designing. Both Bessie and she could sew and if she could make stylish clothes from nothing she reckoned she was suddenly part of the war effort and she had a new interest. For the first time since the war began Ida felt she could cope.

Betty Preston was in love. The day after she had met Ted she was doing some soldering, wearing her protective goggles, and she looked up to find all eyes were upon her. She liked to gossip herself and she knew immediately that they'd been talking about her. Because making munitions was noisy, all the girls became expert lip readers, and she saw one of them mouth, 'You're a dark 'orse.' It didn't bother her that they talked about her. But how did they even *know?*

In the canteen above the noise of *Worker's Playtime* she asked the ringleader a girl called Hazel Perks, 'Why 'ave you bin talkin' about me, Hazel?'

Hazel grinned. 'You knows reet well. You was seen with a bloke last night. Smashin'-lookin' by all accounts and you 'adn't let on to anyone.'

'I likes to keep my business to meself. And who told you?' Betty glanced around the canteen tables, and there sat skinny Hilda Ogden trying not to grin. Betty stood up and walked over to her. ''Ilda Ogden, if you saw me last night why didn't you say 'ello?'

Hilda's mind didn't work quickly enough to answer that one.

'You're like an old woman, 'Ilda,' said Betty. 'All wind and gossip. Say nowt about folk if you don't want them to say owt about you.'

Hilda shrugged. 'At least I've got meself a husband.'

Hazel Perks laughed. 'Gawd, 'Ilda, you're priceless. Is that all you care about?'

'Bet he wears specs, then,' one of the girls said.

''E does not. 'E's right 'andsome and 'e's good to me.'

'What does that mean, 'Ilda? That 'e

bought you a shandy and asked before he took yer knickers off?'

Hilda was off her chair and across the room faster than a rivet from a gun. 'You dirty bitch!' she screamed, as she flew at the girl who'd insulted her. In moments they were on the canteen floor in a heap of arms and legs and a torrent of insults that made Betty cover her ears. No one tried to stop the fight even when Hilda grabbed her opponent by the hair and began banging her head on the table. 'My Stan's an 'ero,' she shrieked, 'and don't you forget it.'

In the group watching, one quiet voice said, ''E'd 'ave to be a ruddy 'ero to marry 'er.'

The fight only broke up when the klaxon sounded for them to get back to work. Betty smiled to herself. A bit shy, she was glad that she was no longer the centre of attention. At least now, though, she felt more like one of the girls than she had before. And Ted had done that for her. You've gone daft, she told herself, when she felt all excited just at the thought of him. He was the reliable type, the sort of man she wanted to marry, and she was seeing him again tonight. Nothing was going to stop her – not her father or her poor mother. Ted was her priority now.

CHAPTER TEN

Spring 1944: Resistance Blows up Hydroelectric Station at Bussy

In her flat at the Glad Tidings Mission Hall Ena was perusing the local paper. Tucked away on the second page she read, 'Missing boys cause concern.' Three boys had run away from a children's home in Manchester. The youngest, Dieter Holliman, aged nine, was thought to be in the Weatherfield area.

Ena slipped on her coat, picked up her umbrella and marched out into the drizzle. When she arrived at Minnie's, Dieter was doing a jigsaw on the floor. The weeks he'd been with Minnie had transformed him, and he looked more like the nine-year-old he was than the six-year-old he had appeared to be when they first met him. 'Hello, Mrs Sharples,' he said. 'Can you do jigsaws? I'm stuck.'

'I'll 'elp you in a minute, lad. After I've 'ad words with Mrs Caldwell.'

Ena pushed Minnie into the scullery and

closed the door. 'It's in the papers,' she said in a whisper.

'What is, Ena?'

'About the lad, you daft cluck.'

'No need to be rude, Ena. I do 'ave feelin's.'

'Aye, but I'm right mithered. It says in the papers 'im and two other lads are missin' from an orphanage. It says they're concerned – mind you, they've done nowt about it till now. 'As 'e told you what happened?'

''E's still scared, Ena. 'E thinks the Nazis will come to take us both away if they find 'im.'

'Don't you fret about that, Minnie Caldwell. 'E'll tell us nowt till 'e thinks it's safe. Don't you forget in all this we've got the Lord on our side.'

'I think I'll just rely on you, Ena.'

'Aye. Well, put kettle on and I'll 'ave a talk wi' the lad.'

'Don't you frighten 'im, Ena,' warned Minnie.

Ena's eyes flashed bright as coal in snow. 'Now, you look 'ere, Minnie Caldwell. If that lad ran away from a bloomin' orphanage he 'ad good reason. And, as I live and breathe, 'e won't be goin' back. I reckon 'e's

159

suffered enough.' She took a breath. 'We just 'ave to work out a plan.'

'I do 'ope so, Ena. I love 'avin 'im 'ere.'

When Ena returned to the back room Dieter looked at her warily. 'Now then, lad,' she said, getting down on the floor with him. 'Let's see if I can 'elp you wi' this jigsaw.' She managed to find two pieces before she said, 'Did they 'ave jigsaws in the 'ome?'

He looked up sharply. 'Did Kenneth tell you?'

Ena shook her head. 'Nay, lad. It's in papers.'

'They're looking for me?'

Ena nodded. 'It's up to you, lad. Do you want to stay in Weatherfield?'

He stared at her, his blue eyes full of fear. 'You won't send me back, will you?'

Ena patted his shoulder. 'Why don't you tell us all about it, lad?'

Dieter stared down at the jigsaw. 'They said I was a bad lot at the orphanage,' he muttered. 'The matron kept locking me in my room. I didn't mind that – I was used to hiding and being on my own.'

'What did you mind, lad?'

'I wet the bed at night and she made me wash the sheets and called me "Dirty Dieter", and then everyone made fun of me.

160

Then she said I was stealing food. I wasn't, Mrs Sharples, honest I wasn't. I only saved bread and put it in my pocket. She hit me with a ruler for that. She said I was a German Jew thief and no one should trust me. There were two other boys she didn't like – big boys – and we decided to run away. They helped me get into the loft and they'd bring me food. I don't where they are now but I wouldn't tell if I knew. It's a horrible place, that home, and it's nice here. Mrs Caldwell lets me save bread and I don't wet the bed any more.'

Ena ruffled his hair. 'What's her name, this matron?'

'Mrs Makins.'

'Well, pet, I don't think you'll be seein' 'er again. There's just one more thing I wants to know, lad. How come you speak such good English?'

His lower lip trembled. 'My mother spoke English and I've been in England since I was three.'

Ena longed to ask what had happened to his mother but she could see tears in his eyes and guessed she was dead. 'Where did you live before the orphanage, Dieter?'

He looked down. 'In London – the East End.' Ena lifted his chin and smiled at him.

'Can I stay here for ever?' he asked.

'As long as you want to. Weatherfield folk will see you right.'

Minnie came in with some bread and jam and tea, and placed the tray on the table. She'd been listening at the door and her insides were twitching like an eel on a plate.

''Ave you come up with a plan, Ena?' she asked.

'Aye. I'll be payin' that 'ome a visit.'

'You won't cause a row, will you?' asked Minnie nervously.

'Row?' said Ena. 'I tell yer this, Minnie Caldwell, that Mrs Makins is going to rue the day she was born. The fear of God is what she'll know. As I've said before, I can't abide them as is cruel to kiddies and them who think they can take advantage of folk who're different.'

'Don't you get yerself in trouble, Ena.'

Ena sipped her tea thoughtfully. 'Don't fret, Minnie. Trouble is comin' *their* way, not mine. Just you wait and see.'

Minnie smiled across at Dieter. She was still worried but she put her faith in Ena. She loved Dieter already, and if Ena needed help then she was more than willing to give it. 'When you go and see that Mrs Makins, Ena, can I come with you?'

162

There was a long pause before Ena said, 'You 'ave a 'eart of gold but I can't see you bein' much 'elp.'

'Why not, Ena? Two of us would be better.'

Ena thought about that. 'Minnie Caldwell,' she said, 'sometimes you're a bloomin' inspiration.'

'Does that mean you do want me 'elp, Ena?'

'You stay on the 'ome front, Minnie, where you belong,' said Ena, slipping on her coat. 'What we need for this is a bit of brawn. The man who's got it don't need brains. I'll do the thinkin' and 'e can look tough.'

The only trouble with Ena's new plan was that she couldn't think of anyone who quite fitted the bill.

Annie Walker had only just recovered from her mortifying experience of being late for opening time then getting caught in a raid. She'd been in a communal shelter twice now. She hated the smell, the snotty-nosed children, and the never-ending gossip, even the forced cheeriness of the communal singing. There were times in the Rovers when she could forget the war was on. Being

163

with a smelly crowd in some dingy shelter *was* the war for Annie. At least, it felt like a battleground. And the gossips at the Rovers had had their field day too. No one had said anything to her but she knew, by the whispers and glances, that they suspected something. She'd written to John and told him that perhaps they shouldn't meet for a while and at long last he'd replied. It had been Teresa who picked up the post that morning.

'Letter for you, Mrs Walker from...' and then she'd smiled in her sly way. Annie's stomach did the polka. She sat down to read the letter. He was missing her. She was his ideal woman and he would do anything to make her happy including leaving Bessie Street and finding a new post in the country. He had enough money for a little house and he would happily take on Annie's children. When she was divorced from Jack they could marry. The word divorce shimmered in front of her eyes. *Divorce*. People like her didn't get divorced. She'd made vows that couldn't be broken.

The letter and Teresa's knowing look unnerved Annie all day, and that evening in the bar she felt particularly tetchy.

'Please wipe your feet and show some

consideration,' she exhorted her customers. When Elsie Tanner came in, flaunting her new boyfriend, she felt even more irritated. A trollop like Elsie Tanner could do what she wanted yet Annie couldn't get back late just once without rumour and gossip.

Elsie and her new man sat together, holding hands and laughing, and Annie felt jealous.

'What's up wi' you, Mrs Walker?'

Ena's voice broke into Annie's thoughts. 'Your usual, Mrs Sharples?'

Ena nodded.

'Is it true what I hear?' asked Annie. 'That you've taken in a young runaway that the authorities are looking for?'

'That's as maybe but it's of no interest to you, is it, Mrs Walker?'

'I'm interested in the welfare of children, and if he's run away he's probably a real troublemaker.'

Ena tried to keep her temper. 'Annie Walker, I'll say nowt to you now but I'll be round for a chat wi' you before opening time in morning. Till then I should say nowt to anyone or you might regret it.'

'Is that a threat, Mrs Sharples?'

Ena paused. 'Aye.'

Annie's hand trembled as she placed Ena's

milk stout on the bar. Some of it spilled and Ena glared at her. 'I like a full measure, Mrs Walker, as I'm reet sure you do.'

'What's that supposed to mean?'

'You wouldn't want me to say anythin' 'ere, would yer?'

Annie topped up the glass and moved on to her next customer. Her legs were shaking so much that she thought her knees would give way. She realized that Ena Sharples knew something that might give her a hold over Annie – *for ever.*

Elsie Tanner finished her third gin and orange and squeezed Antonio's knee. 'I'm 'avin' a lovely time,' she said. 'I 'aven't been so 'appy for ages.'

'I've got a surprise for you, Elsie.'

'You've given me nowt but surprises. What's it this time?'

'I've got two days leave.'

Elsie was delighted. 'You'll stay at my place, won't you?'

'Elsie, darling, where else would I stay?'

'It did cross me mind that an 'andsome bloke like you might 'ave a little Italian wife hidden away.'

He laughed. 'Italian women aren't so little. But I don't have a wife – yet.'

''Ave you got plans, then?'

He took her hand. 'When a certain beautiful woman is free, who knows?'

'Pity there's nowt I can do about my Arnold, then.'

'After the war you can.'

'This ruddy war that we're supposed to be winning goes on and on.'

'Soon it will be over, my Elsie, and then you and I...' He kissed her hand and stared into her eyes.

'Stop it,' she said. 'You make my spine tingle.'

'Don't worry, you'll soon be–' He couldn't finish because a man approached their table.

'I thought you and the Todds were meant to be friends,' said Len Fairclough.

Elsie, a little drunk, merely laughed. 'What's the matter, Len? Someone locked you in the privy?'

Antonio stood up. 'I'm with this lady. What's the problem?'

'That's no lady – that's Elsie Tanner.'

Elsie stood up too. She was angry now. 'What the 'ell 'ave I done to upset you?'

''Ave you bothered to go round and see Dot?'

'Flu's catchin'. I don't want to give it to

my kids, do I?'

Len stared at her. 'You don't mind leavin' them alone while you go out with yer Eyetie boyfriend.' At this Antonio gave him a hefty push. Len staggered on his good leg but didn't fall. 'You bloody foreigner!' he shouted. 'Why aren't you fightin' on yer own side?'

Antonio pushed aside a chair and advanced towards Len, who now had his fists raised. 'I thought you Eyeties were meant to like kids,' bellowed Len. 'It's all right for 'er to leave 'er kids screaming in the dark, is it, so as a neighbour 'as to come in to them.'

Antonio stopped in his tracks. 'Is this true, Elsie?'

Elsie looked ashamed. 'Dot couldn't 'ave 'em and they were asleep.'

Antonio raised his palms to Len. 'Sorry, mister. I'll take her home now.'

Len lowered his fists.

'Elsie, put your coat on,' said Antonio.

'I 'aven't finished me drink yet.'

'Yes, you have.'

'No, I 'aven't.'

He picked up her glass and downed the gin. 'I say you have.'

Elsie lunged at him. 'You've got a bloody

168

nerve,' she screamed. He grabbed her wrist and began pulling her to the door. Elsie kicked him once or twice but he seemed not to notice. As they left, the Rovers erupted into cheering.

Annie Walker, relieved that no damage had been done and that Elsie Tanner had got her comeuppance, gave Len a pint on the house.

'Mrs Walker hasn't done owt like that since 1938,' said Albert Tatlock. 'They must be right – war *is* nearly over.'

Elsie's high heels clattered up the street as Antonio dragged her along. Once in the back alley she shouted, 'You're not me bloody 'usband. And you're 'urtin' me arm.' She didn't care if the neighbours heard.

'Good,' said Antonio, as he pushed her through the back door. 'No wife of mine would leave her children alone. That bloke at the Rovers was right and you should be ashamed of yourself.'

A flustered Bessie Tatlock stood up from a chair. 'I'm just going,' she said. 'They've both gone back to sleep now. Screaming fit to bust, they was.'

She rushed away, leaving Elsie with arms akimbo and Antonio's eyes flashing like a pair of searchlights.

'What I do with my kids is my business,' said Elsie, who had sobered up now. 'Not yours or Len Fairclough's.'

'Perhaps you don't care what happens to them.'

'That does it!' she said, snatching up Dennis's bottle and throwing it at him. He ducked. Then she threw a salt cellar, followed by a bottle of vinegar. Each time they missed. The vinegar bottle smashed against the door, which incensed her more. She threw cushions at him and finally her right shoe.

'Caught you, you sod,' she screamed, as the shoe hit the side of his head. She felt a lot better then, but as Antonio sank slowly to the floor, fear took a grip. He lay on the floor behind an armchair. She rushed to kneel beside him. 'Oh, Gawd, Antonio, wake up! Come on! Speak to me. It were only a shoe.'

There was no sign of a wound but he lay, eyes closed, unmoving. She shook him by the shoulders but there was still no response. She put her ear to his chest to see if his heart was still beating but she wasn't sure if it was her own heart hammering away that she could hear. Just as she lifted her head from his chest his hands grabbed her face, his eyes flicked open and he was staring at her. Elsie's mouth was half open in surprise but not for long. He pulled her to him and began kissing her passionately. She struggled at first but then relaxed as relief mixed with desire flooded through her. Then he rolled her over so that he was on top of her with her arms pinned down and he began to laugh. 'Elsie Tanner – the only woman I know who can throw like that is my mama and she throws like an Italian. I always knew you were the woman for me.'

He kissed her again and Elsie didn't resist this time. Nothing could stop her enjoying herself now – not the kids, not the war, not even her memories of Steve. Nothing mattered except the pleasure. And Antonio was proving he could supply a lot more than fags.

CHAPTER ELEVEN

Spring 1944: Rome Falls to the Allies

Annie Walker had waited for Ena Sharples's visit with real trepidation. When the knock came an hour before opening time she told Teresa to take Billy and Joan out for a walk. One thing she didn't want was any of her conversation being overheard.

'Do take a seat, Mrs Sharples,' she said. 'Would you like some tea?'

Ena was in no mood to be polite. 'I'll mek me point and then I'll be off.'

'And what is your point, Mrs Sharples?'

'I'm not one to make owt of molehills, Annie Walker, but I'd say you've been cutting your privet a bit close to the edge.'

'There's no need to talk in riddles, Mrs Sharples.'

Ena put a hand on her hip and stared at Annie. 'You've been seen,' she said. 'We've all 'ad our suspicions and we know you've got a gentleman admirer.'

Annie wasn't surprised and she decided

her best form of defence was to go on the attack. 'Who I see is none of your business, Mrs Sharples. I do have a gentleman friend, and that's all he is. A true gentleman. I've done nothing to be ashamed of.'

'Your Jack is a real gent, Mrs Walker, don't you forget. 'E's fightin' for you and yours while you're seein' your fancy man.'

Annie, well used to keeping her temper under control, said evenly, 'I can see I have to repeat myself. It's purely my business and I have nothing else to say on the matter.'

'I mek it my business when you start openin' your big gob about that little lad.'

'I was only thinking,' said Annie, 'about what was right and proper.' As soon as the words had left her lips, Annie realized she'd given Ena all the ammunition she needed.

'Right and proper, is it, to send a lad back to a 'ome where 'e was badly treated?' snapped Ena. 'Right and proper, is it, to see a man behind your 'usband's back? Right and proper, is it, not to open Rovers on time? Right and proper...'

Wearily Annie put up her hand. 'You've more than made your point, Mrs Sharples. What is it you want me to do?'

Ena folded her arms across her chest. 'I'm goin' to get that orphanage sorted,' she said, 'but if anyone comes lookin' for 'im you say 'e was in Weatherfield but 'e's gone now. Do you understand? And if we can't get coupons for the lad we might need 'elp to keep feedin' and clothin' 'im.'

'But surely Mrs Caldwell can't plan to keep him for ever?'

'These things 'appen in wartime,' snapped Ena. 'If we can't look after the kiddies there's no bloomin' 'ope for us.'

'Very well, Mrs Sharples. Is there anything more?'

'Just your Jack. I won't be writin' to 'im now, but think on about what's right and proper. You're not Elsie Tanner – she's a trollop and she never did care for that Arnold of 'ers. Your Jack is a good man and 'e deserves an 'ero's 'omecomin', not findin' out his missus 'as been pantin' like a bitch on 'eat for another man. You save your breath for your Jack.'

Tight-lipped, Annie said, 'Thank you so much for your advice. I'd be grateful if we never spoke of this again.'

Ena turned to go. 'Don't think because I'm a widow I don't now nowt about animal passions. I put me passion into servin' the Lord and you'd do well to do the same.'

When Ena had gone Annie Walker went

into the bar and had a quick swig of brandy. She rarely drank alcohol but today she needed a stiffener. The trouble was, she knew that Ena Sharples was right. She'd tried to end it, wanted to, but John was persistent. Too persistent. He had come round after hours and tried to persuade her that her future lay with him. He'd begun writing to her every day. It was easy enough for Ena Sharples to dispense advice but she had a feeling John Barnstable just wasn't going to take no for an answer.

Betty Preston was running out of excuses for going out in the evening. As she walked home from work she realized that a third evening of 'baby sitting' might make her father suspicious, and if Holy Harold found out she had been to dance halls and pubs there would be a holy war. Betty hadn't even told her mother.

When she arrived home her mother was sitting in her armchair looking pale and breathless. 'Are you all right, Mam?' asked Betty.

'I've been movin' about too much. Tried to get the rugs up so I could give 'em a good beatin' in the yard.'

'I always do that, Mam. Just leave it to me.'

Her mother's plump hand grasped Betty's arm, and Betty was shocked to see that Margaret's hair was turning white. She hadn't noticed before. 'You do far too much, Betty,' she said breathlessly. 'Your father only wants to feed me and Bible thump. You won't be here for ever.'

'What do you mean?'

'You know what I mean, my girl. I know you've got a boyfriend.'

'How'd you know?'

'Maggie saw you with 'im.'

'Trust 'er to open her big mouth. If she tells Dad I'll swing for 'er.'

'I'm sure your dad would like you to get married.'

'Oh, yes, Mam. A holy Joe and then a life like–'

'You can say it. A life like mine. I don't want that for you, Betty. Is 'e a nice lad?'

Betty nodded. 'He's perfect, except 'e's a southerner and 'e's no church goer.'

Her mother sighed. 'That'll give your dad a heart attack. Best keep it quiet.'

Betty made Margaret a cup of tea, beat the rugs in the garden and began peeling potatoes. Should she stand up to Harold? What could he do? Clip her ear? If he did that she could run out of the house in a huff. Maybe, she thought, she could say he was from Manchester way, which wasn't a complete lie, and that he was a regular chapel-goer, which was a downright lie.

When her father came in he took one look at Margaret and began blaming Betty. 'Look at the state your mother's in! She should be in bed. Have you given her anything to eat?'

'I'm just getting the tea ready.'

'Well, leave that and get your mother to bed.'

'I don't want to go to bed, Harold,' said Margaret. 'I'm feeling better now.'

'And I know what's best for you. Betty will 'elp you.'

'She's all right, Dad,' protested Betty. 'She was a bit breathless but there's nowt wrong now.'

'I'll be the judge of that. Now do as you're told.'

Betty stared at her father defiantly. 'No.'

'What did you say?'

'I said no, Dad. Mam doesn't want to go to bed.'

Harold advanced towards her menacingly. 'A child doesn't argue with its parents.'

'I'm not a child, I'm a woman.'

'You live under my roof and you'll do as I tell you.'

'Stop it, Harold,' cried out Margaret. 'I can manage on my own.' Harold turned his head to watch his wife lumber to her feet. Her bulk seemed to fill the room but Betty knew that inside the huge frame was a small frightened person. And it was Harold who had made her so.

Margaret made her way slowly up the stairs. Betty stared at her father and for once he looked away. Then she said, 'I'll go up and see to Mam and then I'm going out.' He didn't answer and at that moment Maggie walked in.

'Maggie, go up to Mam,' Betty said. 'She needs 'elp gettin' into bed. I'll see to the tea.'

Maggie looked daggers at Betty but she didn't argue.

Just before Betty went out she looked in on her mother, who lay propped up on several pillows, her face white and beads of sweat on her forehead. She seemed to be asleep, the remains of a plate of liver and onions on the table by her bed. Just as Betty turned to go, her mother's eyes flickered open and she said, 'Whatever 'appens to me, pet, mek sure you leave this 'ouse.'

'Aye, Mam.'

'Promise me.'

'I promise.'

Margaret sighed and murmured. 'You're a good girl.'

Betty met Ted outside the Rovers with a heavy heart and a worried expression.

'What's the matter, Betty, love?' he asked.

'Me mam's not well.'

'Let's 'ave a drink, then, and you can tell me all about it.' He put an arm around her and Betty sensed that if there was one person she could trust with her family secrets it was Ted. And it made her realize that not only did she trust him, she really was in love with him.

When Antonio had left after his leave Elsie Tanner felt that the sunshine had gone with him but at least he'd promised to write to her. She received few letters and sometimes she doubted that Arnold could even write. Antonio's letters would make her feel she was more like the other wives who waited for the postman. She guessed that his family must be rich because most servicemen only earned enough for beer and the odd night out but Antonio always had money.

Elsie had been to the Todds' and gave Sally as much help as she could. The flu had left Dot weak and depressed, but now she was rallying and it was Vi who was giving cause for concern. There was a rumour that she'd got tipsy on a night out with some old friends and had fallen into the canal during the blackout. She'd denied it, saying she'd just got soaked in a downpour. Either way, Dot had sent for the doctor twice but all he could suggest was aspirin and cough linctus. Vi had taken to her bed looking ill and feverish and coughing up blood.

'She won't die, will she, Elsie?' Sally had asked her.

'Your mam is as strong as an ox,' said Elsie. 'There's nowt a bit of a rest won't cure.' But when Elsie went upstairs to say goodbye and saw Vi pale and slack-mouthed, with her chest sounding like a bubbling cauldron, she wasn't so sure.

It was Friday, late afternoon, and Elsie had finished work early. Orders at Elliston's had slackened off and word was that now that the Allies were planning a final push in Europe the workers might have to go on short time. Elsie could just remember the Depression, and with her bit of extra money in her old teapot she felt more secure. She'd paid a girl who used to work at Elliston's to have the kids till Saturday morning and she'd used her clothing coupons to buy a new dress with a low-cut white collar and she wanted Dot to see it. 'Come back with me, Dot, and I'll show you me new dress.'

Dot looked anxiously at Sally. 'Will you be able to manage Mam and your Clark for a couple of hours?'

'Go on, you 'ave a break,' said Sally. 'Mam's asleep and Clark's quiet for once and you 'aven't been out for ages.'

'You've turned into a right little mother hen, our Sal. I'm proud of yer.'

On the way to Elsie's, Dot's worries about Vi surfaced. 'Should I let me dad know?'

'I reckon 'e might get leave,' said Elsie, 'and that might be the tonic she needs.'

'Yeah, you're right Elsie – I'll do that.'

Elsie couldn't wait to show Dot her dress and she stripped off straight away, put it on and waited for Dot's admiration.

'It's reet glamorous, Elsie, shows your figure off a treat. Where did you get the brass for that?'

Elsie smiled. 'Antonio sends me a bit now and again.'

'Where does 'e get it?'

'There's no need to put that expression on your gob, Dot. I'm always givin' you a share of me food and fags.'

'Aye, and I'm grateful, but it makes you

wonder, don't it?'

Elsie shrugged. ''Is folk are in business so they see 'e's all right.'

Dot lit the cigarette that Elsie offered and began to cough at the first puff.

'You're still coughin' for England, Dot. You should pack up.'

'Don't try and gerroff the subject, Elsie. You told me they was in the ice-cream business and I've seen no ice-cream since war began.'

'That's what 'e told me.'

'Well, he wouldn't say owt about black market would 'e.'

Elsie thought about that for a moment. ''Ave you noticed 'ow folk moan about black marketeers but if anything comes their way they pay up and say nowt?'

'Aye. You're right. Bloody 'ypocrites, they are.'

'Anyway,' said Elsie, 'I 'eard from 'im this morning and 'e's got what 'e calls a little "business proposition" for me.'

'What is it, then?' Nothin' against the law I 'ope.'

Elsie shook her head. 'No, it's nowt like that. 'E says as 'ow a lot of his mates 'ave nowhere to go when they're on leave. They get a couple of days and they're stuck at the base. So 'e says could I offer them bed and breakfast? They'd pay me the going rate.'

Dot said thoughtfully, 'Are you sure there's nowt else they'd want?'

'What yer tryin' to say?' asked Elsie suspiciously.

'Don't get me wrong, Elsie, but 'ow would you cope with young 'andsome blokes walking about in their vest and pants?' Dot asked.

'Are you sayin' I've got no control?'

'Well, you ain't exactly a nun, are you?'

Elsie tried to keep a straight face. 'Neither are you, Dot. I don't see as 'ow I'd 'ave a problem.'

'You would if you'd 'ad a few gins.'

Elsie laughed. 'That's not a bad idea. Do yer fancy one now?'

'Does 'Itler need his cronies?'

After two gins Elsie broached the subject of the kids. 'See, Dot, if I 'ad three payin' guests then what would I do wi' kids?'

'You mean, would I 'ave 'em?'

'Or yer mam, and we could give 'er a few bob.'

'Only when me mam's on her feet again. Could be a bit o' fun for us, Elsie. Any road, I'll give you an 'and wi' the washin' and be your chaperone.'

Elsie chortled. 'Three gins, Dot, and you're worse than me. Some chaperone you'd mek.'

'I need a bit of fun, Elsie. I 'aven't heard from Walt in weeks. Sometimes I think I'll never see 'im again.'

'All I 'ope is I never see Arnold again ever.'

'Not likely is it?'

Elsie grimaced. 'It's about as likely as Ena Sharples tekkin' up with Len Fairclough.'

Elsie poured them both another large gin and halfway through they realized she was in no condition to go out. 'Never mind, Dot – soon lads will be comin' to us. We won't 'ave to go far for a dance, will we? I might even get a gramophone.'

Dot giggled. She hadn't felt as good as this since she first set eyes on Sally's baby. At last life was looking up.

Suddenly, an hour later, Sally was banging and screaming at the front door.

Elsie opened it. 'Quick – quick! Get Dot!' Sally shouted, tears streaming down her face. 'Mam's dyin'!'

As the three of them ran, Elsie called, ''Ave you sent for the doc?'

Sally was too choked to answer but she nodded.

In the bedroom Len sat holding Vi's hand. Her face was sunken, her nostrils thin and waxy-looking. Her breathing was loud and strained, and every so often it stopped, to start again with loud gasps. Dot and Sally stood by her bed, crying.

'She can't die,' sobbed Sally. 'I needs 'er. My Clark needs 'er.'

Len stood up stiffly. 'You girls come and sit by your mam and 'old 'er 'ands. I reckon that's what she's waitin' for.'

Elsie and Len left the room. Elsie was in tears too. She couldn't believe Vi was dying. She'd always been so strong and full of life.

An hour later Sally and Dot appeared, red-eyed but a little calmer. 'She's gone, Elsie,' said Dot. 'She's left us.' There seemed to be nothing Len or Elsie could say to comfort them. 'I wish me dad 'ad been 'ere,' said Sally, picking up her sleeping baby and rocking him backwards and forwards. ''E'll blame us – I know 'e will.'

'It's no one's fault,' said Len. 'You did your best. And you were with 'er. That's what matters.'

Ena Sharples sat alongside Martha in the Rovers. ''Ave you bin to that orphanage yet, Ena?' asked Martha, with a touch of sus-

185

picion in her voice.

'Not as yet. There's bin no sign of anyone searchin' for the lad. An' I'm lookin' for a man to go wi' me.'

'Not scared to go on your own, Ena?'

'Don't talk dafter than usual, Martha. I'll tell you summat. If 'Itler 'imself walked in 'ere now I'd be owt but frightened. I'd go for 'im soon as look at 'im.'

''It 'im with your gas mask, would you, Ena?'

'Martha Longhurst, I'd probably pick you up and use you as a bloomin' batterin' ram.'

Martha sipped her milk stout unperturbed. 'You've still not told me owt 'bout this fella you're looking for.'

Ena looked around the bar. 'I've 'eard this Mrs Makins 'as got a big 'usband. She might not let me 'ave my say.'

'By 'eck, Ena, I can't believe that.'

'Are you bein' funny, Martha Longhurst?'

'It's not in my nature to be funny, Ena.'

'Aye. You never said a truer word. Now, where was I afore you poked your oar in?'

'Mitherin' about not 'avin your say.'

'I need a man,' said Ena, casting Martha a glance that would quell a Zulu warrior, 'as'll do as 'e's told but can act tough if needs be.'

'Sounds like a lot of blokes round 'ere.

Not much between their lug-'oles but fists the size of pig's trotters.'

'That's as mebbe. Show me one then.'

Martha looked round the Rovers and found she couldn't prove her point. Albert Tatlock and Tom Hewitt and one or two old boys of the Home Guard were in but not one had muscles bigger than a pigeon's egg. And then the door opened and in walked Stanley Ogden and Hilda.

''Im,' said Martha.

Ena looked around. 'Where?'

Martha nodded in the pair's direction. 'Over there, by the door.'

Ena stared at the pair of them. ''E might do,' she murmured. 'Why didn't I think of 'im before? 'E's easily led if you ask me.' After a few seconds' deliberation she stood up. 'I'll get us another milk stout and see just 'ow much persuading 'e'll need.'

Annie Walker smiled frostily as Ena ordered the drinks. 'This gentleman is first, Mrs Sharples.'

Ena looked Stan up and down. He was tall and broad and he didn't have a pretty face. 'Well, a big fella like you won't barge in front of a poor widow like me, would you, son?'

'No, missus. You go first. I ain't in no 'urry.

Me an' 'Ilda are still celebratin' gettin' married.'

'Well, in that case,' said Ena, 'I'll buy you both a drink.'

'No need, missus. Let me buy you one.'

Ena smiled. 'Aye, lad. You do that. I might just 'ave a little job you can 'elp me with.'

He grinned, and Ena knew she'd found her man.

CHAPTER TWELVE

Spring 1944: Stalin declares: 'The wounded German beast must be pursued and finished off in its lair.'

On the day of Vi's funeral Jack Todd arrived home on compassionate leave and the hearse arrived early to wait outside the front door. The undertakers, in black top hats and tails, carried Vi's coffin out of the house. Jack, with his daughters, walked behind the hearse. Other family and friends fell into step behind them and the slow procession made its way past the occupants of Coronation Street, who stood in silence by their front doors, the men removing their caps, the women nodding their respects.

After the funeral service and the burial, Dot and Sally served tea, ham sandwiches and Madeira cake to the crowd of mourners. Jack drank most of a bottle of whisky and stared morosely into space until he fell asleep.

Dot, now dry-eyed, murmured to Elsie, 'I

don't feel young any more. Me mam bein' gone 'as changed everything.'

'I know, pet.'

'I'll do me best for Sally and our dad.'

'I know you will,' said Elsie. 'And I bet your mam is lookin' down from 'eaven at this very minute feeling reet proud of you both.'

'I do 'ope so.'

'What was it she used to say when you 'ad a moan?'

Dot smiled. '"If there's nowt you can do then you just 'ave to put up and shut up."'

'You can't argue with that, Dot,' said Elsie. 'Shall we 'ave a proper drink now?' She pushed Dot nearer to the sideboard, where there was a bottle of port and a half bottle of gin. 'A toast for your mam,' she said.

They toasted Vi with gin and orange squash. 'Mam did love a gin,' said Dot.

'We'll 'ave to 'ave a few more, then,' suggested Elsie.

Dot smiled. 'Any excuse, Elsie Tanner!' and suddenly they were both laughing. And Dot knew, sure as sure, that somewhere peaceful her mother was laughing with them.

'Nice 'ere,' commented Stanley Ogden, as

he and Ena stood outside The Gables Orphanage on the outskirts of Manchester. The detached house, with neat lawns and apple trees on both sides, was a big contrast to the cramped terraces of Coronation Street.

'There's nowt nice about this place,' said Ena. 'Now, remember, Stanley Ogden, you say nowt but keep your face set, like there were 'ordes of 'Uns comin' at yer.'

'Aye. I'll do me best, Mrs Sharples.'

As they stood on the porch Ena said, 'You've bin on a long leave, Stanley. When are you goin' back exactly?'

Stanley looked at his feet and mumbled something Ena didn't catch.

'You've gone AWOL, you daft beggar, 'aven't yer?'

'Aye,' he said. ''Ilda wanted to get married.'

'Your 'Ilda's not the one in the army, is she? Now, you get back to where you're supposed to be today or the MPs will come for yer.'

'What about 'Ilda?'

Before Ena had a chance to reply, the front door was opened by a girl of about fourteen, wearing a floral apron. She didn't say a word, just looked them up and down and beckoned them in. Inside the door there were two lines of hooks and dozens of coats of different sizes. Underneath were children's boots and shoes. The hall floor was covered in brown linoleum and the walls were a dull green. There were two paintings of mountains and not a sound of a child.

The silent girl led them to a waiting room and pointed to the chairs. A door with a sign, saying *Mrs Makins, Matron* faced them. Ena didn't speak; she was rehearsing in her mind what she was going to say.

A little girl of about two toddled in and walked across to Stanley, looked at him briefly, said, 'Daddy,' and climbed on to his lap. The silent girl appeared suddenly from nowhere to scoop up the child, who began screaming loudly enough to shatter glass. The girl didn't seem to notice.

Mrs Makins appeared then. She was tall and thin with straggly grey hair, and wearing a white overall that made her look like a butcher. Ena also noticed she looked exhausted, the black rings under her eyes and sallow complexion suggesting that she never saw any sunshine.

Ena wasted no time in telling her why they were there. 'It's about Dieter Holliman. You've bin lookin' for 'im.'

Mrs Makins managed a smile. 'Thank goodness for that. I was beginning to think he'd never be found. We heard he was in Weatherfield but no one there could tell us anything.'

'Goodness has nowt to do with it.'

'What's that supposed to mean – and who are you anyway?'

'I'm the caretaker of the Glad Tidings Mission Hall, Mrs Ena Sharples, and this 'ere is Sergeant Stanley Ogden.'

'You'd better sit down and tell me what all this is about.'

Matron Makins sat behind a desk in a wing-back chair. Ena sat stiffly on an upright chair and the newly promoted Stanley stood to attention by her side. 'We might know where young Dieter is,' said Ena.

Mrs Makins seemed pleased. 'That's wonderful. I'll get someone to collect him at once.'

'You'll do no such thing,' retorted Ena. 'Dieter is reet 'appy where 'e is. There's nowt could even drag 'im back 'ere.'

'Why ever not?'

''E says you were cruel to 'im.'

'What absolute nonsense!' snapped Mrs Makins. 'Everything I did was standard procedure.'

'I bet that's what the Nazis say when they're killin' folk.'

'Don't be so ridiculous.'

Ena stood up slowly and deliberately, walked over to the desk and planted her hands firmly on it. 'Don't you call me ridiculous!' she snapped. 'You ill-treat a Jewish kiddie who's probably escaped from who knows what and you've got the bloomin' cheek to call me ridiculous.'

'I wasn't aware that I was mistreating him.'

'There's nowt as stupid as those who 'ave a bit of power.'

Mrs Makins stood up. 'This is getting us nowhere. I think you should leave *now*.'

'We'll leave when we're ready, Mrs Makins,' said Ena. 'Stanley, guard the door.'

Stanley marched to the door and stood blocking it. His face was expressionless.

'I want that lad's papers and his ration books,' demanded Ena.

'Mrs Sharples, you can't possibly have those. It's against the law.'

'Is cruelty against the law?'

'We're going round in circles. I shall be forced to fetch the police.'

'Aye. Mebbe that's a good idea and then we could ask the kiddies 'ere how you treat 'em. I reckon you could be sacked.'

At the mention of being sacked, Mrs Makins's face paled and she slumped back in her chair. She muttered, 'I may have been wrong about Dieter but he was stealing food and bed-wetting. There are thirty-five children here and they have all had terrible experiences. If they all stole food and wet the bed, how would we cope? It's hard enough as it is. I can't get staff. Some young women have joined up and the others work in munitions for half-decent wages. Sometimes I'm here on my own. The girl who let you in works here now. She's been struck dumb ever since her parents died when their house was bombed. That was in 1941.'

Ena's indignation lessened as she began to recognize that this woman was a nervous wreck. 'How come these kiddies can't be evacuated to the countryside?'

Mrs Makins sighed deeply. 'They aren't wanted – they have too many problems. Some were evacuated but they were sent on here. I do my best but I don't think I can carry on.'

For once Ena fell silent. After a few moments she said, 'Young Dieter's very 'appy where 'e is. He's put on weight and 'e wants to go to school. But we need 'is papers. If you write something down about 'im being evacuated to Weatherfield then there'll be nowt for anyone to worry about.'

Mrs Makins rubbed a hand wearily across her forehead and said, 'Very well. But I would appreciate it if you brought him to see me so that I can see he's well.'

'Aye, if and when 'e's willin'.'

While Mrs Makins searched in the filing cabinet for his papers and ration book, Ena said, ''Ow did he get here, any road?'

Mrs Makins paused in her search. 'It seems,' she said, 'his mother worked as a translator as her English was so good. She managed to get out of Germany before war broke out. Her husband, a doctor, planned to follow her later. She took Dieter to the East End of London and they stayed in a house with relatives of hers. The house was bombed – they usually went to a shelter but someone was ill so they stayed at home. Dieter was the only survivor. He was in severe shock for weeks and they kept him in hospital. He only said one word – 'Manchester' – so the authorities presumed he had relatives in the city. We had a vacancy so they sent him here.'

'Poor little mite,' muttered Ena.

'They're all poor little mites,' said Mrs

Makins, handing Ena the ration book. Then she took up a pen to sign the evacuation order. She paused, 'I do hope this is the last I shall hear of these allegations.'

'Just sign the bloomin' thing and we can be off.' Ena held out her hand for the order, then tucked the papers in her handbag. 'Mebbe this is the last you'll 'ear of us, Mrs Makins. Depends on 'ow you go on. If you 'its a child again or meks their life a misery you think on this. The good Lord is watchin' yer and I meself could come back 'ere wi' Stanley and set about *you* wi' a ruler.'

Mrs Makins said nothing.

'Come on, Stanley,' said Ena, 'tek that look off yer face. You look as if you've got a poker up yer bum.'

On the way home Ena felt well satisfied with her efforts. It had been a good morning's work but the other orphans worried her. ''Ow many more will there be after this war is over, Stanley?'

Stanley stopped in his tracks. 'More what, Mrs Sharples?'

'Never mind, Stanley. There's nowt you can do. You'll just do yer bit and 'elp to mek more widows and orphans.'

'Aye,' said Stanley. 'I just does as I'm told.'

Ida Barlow and Bessie Tatlock's make-do-and-mend group now included Minnie Caldwell and Martha Longhurst. Minnie had sorted out some old clothes that had belonged to her late husband, Armistead, that she hadn't had the heart to get rid of. Now, with his trousers and jackets cut down and remade, Dieter had some new clothes. Martha could sew, but her main aim was not to make do and mend but to collect gossip and recycle it.

Elise Tanner's appearance late one Thursday afternoon was a surprise to them all.

'I wonder if you could 'elp me, Ida and Bessie,' she said. 'I've 'eard you can do wonders with a needle and cotton.' They expected a bag full of clothes but Elsie placed a bag of bedding on the table. 'It's sheets, pillowcase and counterpanes,' she explained. 'I was wonderin' if you could turn the sheets sides to middle and patch me pillowcases, and there's a couple of Arnold's shirts that need the collars turnin'.'

Martha Longhurst was quick off the mark. 'Your Arnold comin' 'ome then, is 'e?'

''E'd be as welcome as ruddy snow in August,' said Elsie cheerfully. 'I'll pay you, of course. I can't sew a button on without 'elp so you'll save me life if you freshen up me sheets.'

'Aye, we'll do that,' said Ida. 'Take us two or three days.'

'That'll do grand,' said Elsie. 'I don't need 'em till Monday. Can't stop. Thanks. Ta-ra.'

'Well,' said Martha even before Elsie had gone through the back door, 'what do you mek of that?'

'Spring-cleanin', that's all,' said Ida.

'Elsie Tanner, spring-clean?' sneered Martha. 'She's the sort of woman who does 'er washin' on a Sunday.'

'She does go to work,' said Bessie.

Martha began to undo the bundle of bed-clothes. 'These sheets 'ave seen nowt like starch since she got 'em. Does she call them white? And they got more 'oles in 'em than a colander.'

'We'll do a bit o' patchin',' said Bessie, 'and give 'em a good boiling and a bit o' starch and they'll be as good as new.'

'What I'd like to know,' said Martha, 'is who she wants to impress. I reckon she must 'ave a new man.'

You always think the worst of people, Martha,' said Minnie quietly.

Martha squared her shoulders. 'Chamberlain thought the best of 'Itler and look what 'appened. 'E invaded Poland.' She continued the unpicking she'd started but her heart wasn't in it. 'I shall 'ave to go – I've just remembered summat.'

'What might that be, Martha?' asked Minnie.

Martha frowned at her. 'Just a bit of private business, Minnie Caldwell. I'll catch yer later.'

Martha made her way direct to the Glad Tidings Mission Hall, where she found Ena polishing the chairs. 'Guess what, Ena, I've got a bit o' news.'

'So 'ave I, Martha Longhurst. You put kettle on and I'll tell yer.'

'But–'

'You can tell us in a minute, Martha. Put the kettle on.'

Martha did as she was told, mumbling, 'Are you sure you're not related to someone in Berlin?'

Ena didn't hear. She had troubles of her own.

At the Rovers, Annie Walker and Ned Narkin were clearing up and washing glasses.

'You lock up at the back, Ned,' Annie said.

'I allus do,' he said sullenly.

Annie was wiping the bar when she heard footsteps behind her. She assumed it was Ned but when a voice said, 'Annie,' she almost jumped out of her skin.

'John! You nearly gave me a heart-attack. Did Ned see you?'

'Come out from behind the bar where I can see *you*.'

'You shouldn't come here after hours, John,' said Annie, walking towards him. 'It's not right, and that Ned is a sly old beggar.'

'Ned's gone home now. We're all alone. Perhaps I could have a drink while I'm here.'

Annie poured him a whisky and herself some sherry and as they sat together in the Snug, John took her hand. 'Please, Annie, I know we could be happy together. Why won't you even consider leaving this place?'

'I'm always thinking about it. I haven't heard from Jack in weeks. He may even have been taken prisoner.'

'You'd have heard if he had been.'

Annie shrugged. 'These things happen. We're meant to be winning the war but I don't see any sign of it.'

'I'm trying to win you over, Annie,' he said, stroking her hair, 'and I don't see much response.'

'I'm sorry, John. You mustn't come here again. Too many people know. I've already been threatened.'

'Who by?'

'An old harridan called Ena Sharples. She says she'll write to Jack if I divulge something I know about.'

'What do you know?'

'I'd best not say.'

'If it's about that German lad,' said John, 'he's now a pupil at Bessie Street. He's officially an evacuee staying with a Mrs Caldwell.'

Annie breathed a sigh of relief and at long last smiled at John. He put his arm around her and began kissing her.

'John, you mustn't. No,' she protested. But he continued to kiss her and his hand found her knee. 'No, John,' she said again but it was such a weak protest he didn't hear.

Neither of them heard Teresa walk into the bar and then towards the Snug. 'Mrs Walk–' The girl's mouth dropped open in shock. Hastily Annie rearranged herself. 'What on earth is it, Teresa?'

Teresa glanced away, her face as flushed as Annie's. 'It's the children, Mrs Walker. They've got lice.'

CHAPTER THIRTEEN

Summer 1944: Allied Bombers Wreck Coastal Fortifications Between Cherbourg and Le Havre

Elsie Tanner staggered slightly as she made her way upstairs. She'd been out dancing with Dot but had spent most of the time drinking. The kids were staying overnight with Sally, and Elsie was looking forward to a quiet night. She'd just got into bed when someone started banging on the front door. She leaned out of the front window to see two sailors and a soldier on her doorstep. 'What the 'ell's goin' on?' she yelled.

'Mrs Tanner,' yelled one of the sailors. 'Your 'Tonio said you'd put us up.'

'Oh, Gawd,' muttered Elsie, grabbing her housecoat and rushing downstairs.

She opened the door and saw one or two curtains twitching. 'Sorry we couldn't let you know, love,' said the taller sailor. 'We didn't know ourselves until three hours ago. All hush-hush but it's to do with the invasion plans.'

'Come on in, lads,' said Elsie, 'and mek yerselves at 'ome.'

The arrival of her paying guests had sobered Elsie up, and as they put down their rucksacks and sank into her armchairs she realized just how much room they were going to take up. 'What's yer names, then, lads?' she asked.

'I'm Jack,' said the sailor who had spoken to her at the door. He had blue eyes and thick dark hair. 'This is Eddie Barnes, me shipmate, and in the corner is Jimmy Lawrence from bonny Scotland.' Eddie smiled shyly. He was young, only about twenty, but already he had tired eyes and a worried frown. Jimmy, the soldier, was broad with a wide face and a broken nose. He'd opened his rucksack and now produced a bottle of whisky. 'Ha'e you got some glasses, lass?' he asked, with a grin.

Two doubles later, Elsie remembered she had no sheets on the beds and it was far too late to disturb Ida Barlow. 'Dinnae worry, hen,' said Jimmy. 'A few more wee tots and we'll no' need sheets. We'll sleep like bairns where we sit.'

Jack laughed, 'And Eddie 'ere could sleep on a hammock during action stations if he's 'ad enough to drink.'

Eddie smiled again at Elsie. She couldn't help noticing that he kept glancing at her then looking away.

They talked until the early hours. Eventually Jack and Jimmy fell asleep in the armchairs while Elsie and Eddie continued smoking, drinking and chatting. 'I think you're lovely,' he said suddenly. Drunkenly Elsie ruffled his hair. 'I've never 'ad a girlfriend,' he murmured, 'never 'ardly kissed a girl. I don't suppose I will now. I've lost so many mates who were the same as me. They never 'ad no time either. Now we're goin' to start the invasion and I bet I miss out altogether.'

'I'll give you a kiss,' said Elsie.

'Will you?'

'Aye. Why not?'

She kissed him and afterwards he sighed deeply. 'That were lovely,' he said. 'That's the best thing that's 'appened to me since I joined up.'

Elsie smiled. 'You come with me, lad,' she murmured. 'I can show you summat better than that.'

She took his hand and led him to her bed. 'Your boat's just come in, Eddie,' she whispered in his ear, 'and a reet safe 'arbour it's found.'

Early Saturday morning Ena Sharples joined the queue at the Corner Shop hoping to buy sugar. Martha was way ahead of her in the line but she left her place to join Ena. 'Have you 'eard, Ena?'

'I've 'eard nowt, Martha Longhurst. What are yer on about?'

'Elsie Tanner.'

'What's she bin up to now?'

'I'm surprised you haven't 'eard, Ena.'

'Martha Longhurst, do you keep that beret on your 'ead to keep your brain warm? 'Cos if yer do it's doin' yer no good.'

'Do yer want to know or not?'

Ena shrugged. She was always annoyed when Martha got hold of a bit of news before her and especially annoyed when she made a meal of telling her. 'Just tell us and be done wi' it.'

'Men,' said Martha. 'Servicemen. That's why she wanted 'er sheets patched up.'

'Do you know, Martha Longhurst, you could mek a bloomin' mystery of the Second Coming? You know reet well that men and Elsie Tanner is as common as a bit o' drippin' on toast.'

'They're stayin' there,' announced Martha loudly. 'The three of 'em. Two sailors and a

206

soldier. I reckon they're payin' guests.'

'Payin' guests? Payin' guests! Were you born, Martha, or did you creep out from under a bit o' rhubarb? If she's got men stayin' there she's running a brothel.'

'Do you think so, Ena?'

'I've just said so, 'aven't I. You can stay 'ere and get me sugar and some barm cakes. I'm off to see Elsie Tanner.'

Martha opened her mouth to protest but Ena was already marching off in the direction of No. 11.

She banged hard on the door. 'Elsie Tanner,' she yelled, 'I want words wi' you.'

The door opened suddenly and Ena was faced with the hairy chest of a man otherwise naked but for socks and a towel. 'Och, woman, there's no need to break down the door,' said Jimmy.

'Where's Elsie Tanner?'

'She's away in the Land of Nod, missus. We 'ad a bellyfull last night.'

'Aye, well, give 'er a message from me.'

'Aye, I will.'

'You just tell 'er 'er Arnold will 'ear of this.'

'Who's Arnold?' asked Jimmy.

'Arnold is 'er 'usband.'

Jimmy shrugged. 'Nae harm's done,

woman. Be off wi' ye or I'll show ye what I keep under ma sporran.'

Ena left hurriedly. She knew only too well that the curtains of Coronation Street were twitching as fast as a chicken with its throat cut. And she wasn't prepared to be a laughing stock. There was no doubt that she had to do something, not tomorrow or the next day but this instant.

Back at the Mission she put pen to paper – twice. She had a duty to the children. It was best men knew what was going on on the home front. It would give them a chance to put things right. It was her Christian duty and nothing would deter her.

Elsie Tanner woke up with a start. She opened her eyes and stared at the fair head on the pillow beside her. Who the hell are you? she wondered, until her memory came flooding back. She had no regrets – he'd told her it was the best experience of his life and he'd always be grateful. Then he'd gone to sleep like a baby and still slept although it was past ten.

It was Jimmy who changed her contented mood. 'Some old biddy came round,' he told her, 'threatenin' to tell your 'usband.'

Elsie drank a cup of scalding tea and

dressed quickly. She powdered her nose, used her lipstick as rouge and put plenty on her lips. Only then did she feel ready for the battle. She strode towards the Glad Tidings Mission Hall and hoped the neighbours saw her. In fact, she'd rather Ena came out into the Street for the row just so that everyone could hear what she had to say.

Disappointed to find the door open, she walked in and found Ena with a brush in her hand. 'Just flown in on yer broomstick, 'ave yer?'

'I'm glad you've come, Elsie Tanner. I was at your place today but you didn't 'ave the brass neck to speak to me. I suppose as usual you 'ad nowt on.'

Elsie advanced towards her. 'So 'elp me, Ena Sharples, I'll bloody swing for you.'

Ena pointed the broom handle threateningly. 'Don't you come any closer. I've no scruples about clobbering yer wi' this.'

'What exactly is your gripe wi' me?' demanded Elsie.

Ena lowered the broom slightly. 'There's nowt so sly as a painted Jezebel and that's what you are. You're a married woman with kiddies and every week you're at the post office collectin' your 'usband's wages and now you're–'

'I'm what? Come on, it's not like you to beat about the bloody bush.'

Ena took a deep breath. 'You're a ... prostitute and you're runnin' ... a brothel.'

Elsie stared hard at her adversary then burst out laughing. 'I wish I'd thought of that, Mrs Sharples. You see, I don't sell meself, I gives it away for nowt.' She carried on laughing and Ena grew red in the face.

'You've got no shame, woman,' she bellowed.

Elsie stopped laughing and glared defiantly. 'You're right, Ena "Holier than Thou" Sharples. I enjoys meself which is more than can be said for you. I reckon your Vera is the result of an Immaculate Conception.'

'Don't you bring my Vera into this. She's a respectable girl.'

Elsie laughed. 'Aye, she may 'ave been innocent once but she's not married yet.' Vera was Ena's Achilles heel and Elsie knew that, just as Ena knew that Arnold was Elsie's. All's fair, thought Elsie, especially in war. Love didn't come into it.

'If my Vera's up to owt I wants to know,' said Ena in a calmer voice.

Elsie sensed she was getting the upper hand. 'If I was you I'd get 'er and that Bob

Lomax down aisle as soon as you can.'

'She's not...?' Ena couldn't bring herself to say the word.

'She would be if I 'adn't told 'er what's what.'

'If you ask me,' said Ena, 'it was you who led 'er astray.'

'Don't talk ruddy daft, Ena Sharples. It was me who found 'er on Red Rec allotments in one of the 'uts. If it weren't for me your Vera would be goin' up aisle fit to bust 'er dress.'

'It was 'im, then, who took advantage of 'er,' said Ena, her voice wavering. 'He looks as if butter wouldn't melt if he bloomin' sat on it.'

'Aye,' said Elsie. 'But 'e's still a man. And your Vera is woman enough to 'ave 'ad 'er wicked way with 'im.'

''Ow dare you, Elsie Tanner? My Vera wouldn't–'

'Don't kid yerself,' said Elsie. 'Your Vera isn't a frigid old busybody like you. And I'd be grateful if you didn't write to my Arnold. 'E's quite 'appy and you know 'ow much trouble it caused last time you stuck your oar in.'

''E 'as a right to know.'

'The man is an animal. Don't forget 'e's a

soldier and 'e's more than up to killing me and the kids. He raped me and beat me up. 'E could 'ave killed me then. If you write to 'im, anythin' that 'appens will be on your conscience till the day you die.'

Ena could feel the colour drain from her face. 'There's summat you should know,' she mumbled. 'I've already sent the letter.'

'You stupid old cow!' screamed Elsie, flying at Ena, pulling her turban off and slapping and kicking for all she was worth. Ena fought back and they struggled together on the floor of the Mission Hall. They rolled over and over, not seeing the bucket of dirty water with which Ena had washed the floor. Rolling in the water made no difference, hands clutched at wet hair instead of dry. Elsie managed to slap Ena around the ear and bang her head on the floor.

'Stop it at once.' The weak voice of Mr Swindley caused barely a pause in the fight. When he got no response he ran out of the Mission Hall to get reinforcements.

He came back with Len Fairclough. Len hobbled over and grabbed Elsie's arm. She lashed out at him. 'I'll land you one, Elsie, if you don't stop,' he yelled.

The anger in his voice finally got through

to her. 'Let me go, Len. Let me 'ave one last swing at 'er.'

'You're comin' 'ome now,' said Len, pulling her towards the door. 'You've not changed since you were at school,' he said. 'You got into as many scraps then as a drunken sailor.'

Elsie, wet and breathless, said nothing. She could hear Mr Swindley berating Ena for besmirching the Mission's good name. The last words Elsie heard were, 'You should be thoroughly ashamed of yourself, Mrs Sharples.'

Ena didn't answer. Elsie considered she'd had a victory because if Len hadn't pulled her away she'd definitely have won.

But by the time Len had marched her down the street, Elsie's bravado was weakening, and as she approached her front door she was near to tears. The thought of Arnold returning to create havoc was a real worry. Elsie hadn't exaggerated when she'd told Ena Arnold could kill when he was drunk. He was a nasty piece of work and he was the one person in the world who scared Elsie.

Ena sat in the vestry her head in her hands. When she took her hands away little clumps of hair fell out. That didn't worry her. It was what she'd done that worried her. The letters had gone – it was too late to change that – and now she was full of apprehension and regret. Act in haste, she thought, repent at leisure. If anything happened to Elsie's children she'd never forgive herself.

CHAPTER FOURTEEN

6 June 1944: The D-Day Landings

Like everyone else, Dot Greenhalgh and Elise Tanner had known that some sort of invasion was planned but they hadn't realized the effect it would have. Overnight, it seemed, servicemen disappeared from Weatherfield. There were no dances and paying guests were a thing of the past, while most factories stepped up production.

Dot and Elsie went to the pictures to catch up on the news, but the cinemas were nearly empty and they were forced to buy their own drinks in the Rovers afterwards. On the night of the D-Day landings even Ena Sharples was absent from the Snug.

'Just as well she's not 'ere,' said Elsie sipping her port and lemon. 'Mood I'm in I'd be ready for another go at 'er.'

'It's only 'cos you're mithered about your Arnold,' said Dot. 'With any luck 'e'll 'ave copped it on one of them beaches in Normandy.'

Elsie looked at Dot's expression to see if she was joking. 'I don't wish 'im any 'arm,' she began. '

'I know that,' interrupted Dot, 'but there's a lot of women 'round 'ere who've got mixed feelings 'bout which bloke they wants to see come 'ome.'

'You for one, Dot.'

'Aye,' she said. 'I 'aven't seen my Walt for so long I've forgotten what 'e looks like. The couple of leaves 'e's 'ad 'aven't been so grand. 'E slept most of 'is last twenty-four-hour leave.'

'There'll be no leave for a while and not much going on,' said Elsie, looking at the few old men in the bar. 'What'll we do?'

'Gawd knows,' laughed Dot.

As Elsie was buying another drink a tall man wearing a black overcoat came to the bar. 'Excuse me,' he said to Annie Walker, 'I'm looking for Mrs Ena Sharples.'

'She's not come in yet,' said Annie.

'Are you expecting her?'

Annie looked at him carefully. He was clean and well dressed, although the black overcoat looked strange in summer. He wasn't local, that was for sure, for his accent sounded foreign. Annie was wary. Ena Sharples might have been a thorn in her side but she *was* local and it was always best to be wary of strangers. 'She'll probably be in soon. Would you like a drink while you wait?'

'No, thank you.'

Annie wanted to question him but he smiled and left.

Elsie was intrigued. 'I wonder what 'e wants with Ena Sharples,' she said to Dot.

'I thought 'e looked like the ruddy Grim Reaper,' her friend replied.

Elsie chuckled. 'There's nowt like a bit of 'ope, is there?'

Ena didn't appear that evening and it was two days later that she came in with Martha and Minnie.

'Mrs Sharples,' said Annie, eager to see her reaction, 'there's been a strange man looking for you.'

'Did he want owt?' snapped Ena.

'I really couldn't say. He just asked for Mrs Ena Sharples.'

''E must 'ave said more 'an that.'

'No, that's all, but I had a feeling he might have been from the orphanage.'

'Oh, you did, did you Annie Walker? Dieter is stayin' with Minnie Caldwell, all legal, like, and we 'ave papers to prove it.'

Standing alongside them with an empty half-pint glass in his hand, Albert Tatlock overheard every word. ''E was in Corner Shop two days past. 'E said as 'ow 'e was looking for the little lad. Mrs Foyle lied like a trooper and said there were no spare little lads in Weatherfield.'

'Well,' said Ena. 'I'm glad someone round 'ere 'as got some sense.'

'I reckon 'e's gone now,' said Albert. 'I 'aven't seen 'im since.'

Ena breathed a sigh of relief. 'I 'ope no one says owt about this to Minnie. She dotes on that lad.'

Back in the Snug Ena swore Martha to secrecy. She nodded solemnly and then dropped a bombshell of her own. 'Is it true, Ena, your Vera's getting married in a church?' Ena nearly choked on her milk stout. 'Whoever told you that, Martha Longhurst, is an out-and-out liar. My Vera will be married at the Mission and very soon.'

Martha was silent.

'Well?' demanded Ena.

'Well what?'

'Who told you?'

Martha stared into her glass. 'I 'eard it in a queue. Didn't recognize the voice. Just said she'd 'eard she was 'avin' banns read.'

Ena stood up, threw her tin helmet over her shoulder and said, 'You finish me drink. I'm goin' 'ome to wait for my Vera and see if she's got owt to say for herself.'

Mrs Stanley Ogden stared out of the window of the room she'd shared only four times with her husband since their wedding. Her dad had let them have the front bedroom, but Hilda had soon realized that she couldn't afford to keep Stanley for long: he couldn't use his ration books here and, anyway, being AWOL he wouldn't get paid. With the D-Day invasion starting she was sure the war would be over in a couple of months.

Hilda thought back to Stanley's last morning with her. She'd woken at about six, with Stanley fast asleep and snoring beside her. She'd snuggled down beside him, resting her cold feet on his calves. But she couldn't sleep. 'Stanley? Stanley, are you awake?' she'd asked. He fidgeted. 'Are you awake, Stanley?' she'd repeated.

'I am now. Can't you let a man rest.'

'It's time you went back to your barracks. War's nearly over.'

Stanley had opened one eye. 'Who told yer that?'

'Everyone's sayin' it. Now we're over there the Germans will just give up.'

''Ilda you're talkin' out of the top of your 'ead. Now let me get some kip.'

'You'll 'ave to get a job then.'

'Do give over, woman. 'Ow can I get a job? I've got service papers. I'd be caught in a day.'

'Me dad says we can't afford to keep yer much longer – you eats too much.'

Stanley groaned and sat up in bed. 'I'll stop eatin' then.'

'Don't talk daft. There's no need for that. You'll just 'ave to give yerself up.'

'Aye,' said Stanley, with a deep sigh, 'but there's nowt you know about the glass-house. It's bloody 'orrible. Up at six, march everywhere at the double, bread and water if you do owt wrong and I'd be there months and bloody months.'

'No need to swear, Stanley.'

'Sometimes, 'Ilda, you're enough to make a saint swear.'

'You can't lay low for ever, Stanley.'

''Ilda, I've 'ad a thought.'

'What?'

'I'll join the French bloody Foreign Legion if you're so keen to get rid of me.'

'It's not that, pet, it's me dad.'

Stanley sat on the side of the bed. 'It comes to summat when yer new bride wants yer out of the road.'

Hilda was about to disagree when banging had started on the front door. She had jumped out of bed, run to the window and seen three burly Military Policemen standing on the front door step. 'Run! Stanley, run!' she'd shouted in panic. Stanley paused for only a second and began looking for his trousers, but Hilda gave him no chance. 'Quick – out the back and over the fence,' she said, giving him a shove. Stanley, in vest and underpants, had made it only to the back gate. He was stopped by an MP as wide as the back gate itself.

'I think you're improperly dressed son,' he'd boomed, 'especially for the glasshouse.'

Stanley was led back inside and allowed to get dressed. Hilda glared at the policemen. 'My Stanley was 'ere lookin' after me and if you big lugs 'urt 'im you'll 'ave me to reckon with.'

'Ooh, missus, I'm all of a tremble,' said one.

Hilda wasn't deterred. 'I'm a pregnant woman, and Stanley 'ere was 'avin' to stay with me as I was reet ill.'

'Regular little paragon, ain't 'e?' he said,

smirking at Stanley, then added, 'Get your mouth closed, Ogden, and your boots on.'

'Did you 'ear me?' Hilda demanded.

'Now, look 'ere, missus, keep your lip buttoned. You don't look much fatter than a wax taper so with a bit of luck your man 'ere will be out of the glasshouse by the time it's born.'

''E's my 'usband,' said Hilda indignantly.

When one of the policemen laughed at that, Hilda felt like crying, but she didn't give into it. 'I 'ave a right to kiss 'im good-bye.'

'You've got no rights, sweet'eart, but you can. Make it quick.' Hilda kissed Stanley who was now dressed in his khaki uniform and standing to attention. 'Be brave, pet,' she whispered in his ear.

'Right, Ogden. You know the drill,' shouted the MP with stripes on his arm. 'Left, right. Left, right, left, right.'

It had been a whole two weeks before she had heard any more from Stanley. He was given a month's sentence and was then to go straight back to his unit. 'You're a wonderful woman, Hilda,' he wrote. He also said he was 'behaving himself' but he missed his beer. 'See you soon, chuck,' were his last words.

Hilda left her bed and stared out of the window. It was a pity, she thought, that he hadn't gone AWOL for longer. He was much safer in the glasshouse. Anything might happen to him once he got back to the front.

Albert Tatlock prided himself on being the Weatherfield war correspondent. As an ARP warden he considered it his duty to be well informed on the war's progress. He read the newspapers avidly and listened to the BBC news on the wireless. He took some of the gung-ho propaganda with a pinch of salt but on 13 June, when the first V1 rockets hit London, he felt a real need to talk it over with somebody other than Bessie. She was convinced the war would be over in weeks and then Beattie could come back to them. Albert felt that unless the RAF could find and bomb the rocket sites then the V1s would be a major setback.

'What do you think, Tom?' he asked Tom Hewitt in the Rovers at lunchtime.

'Blowed if I know. But I feel sorry for the poor beggars in London.'

'Strikes me,' said Albert, 'these doodle-bugs can't get up 'ere – not enough fuel.'

Tom, who'd seen the carnage in the First

World War and had learned to take nothing for granted in both war- and peacetime, said dourly, 'The Krauts are clever sods. Them rockets are too fast for radar to pick 'em up and the ack-ack guns too bloomin' slow. You mark my words, this war is far from over. There'll be thousands killed yet.'

Albert had a feeling he was right. ''Ow's your 'Arry doing?' he asked, to change the subject. 'I don't 'ear that often,' said Tom. 'When 'e does come 'ome on leave 'e's as miserable as sin. 'E 'ardly leaves the 'ouse, says the girls don't want to know the local lads, they only want the Yanks.'

Albert nodded. 'They want their nylons and chewing-gum any road. When war's over and Yanks 'ave gone it'll be a different story.'

'I 'ope so,' said Tom. 'I'd like to see our 'Arry settle down before I peg it.'

'There's nowt wrong with you, is there?'

'War weary, that's what I am, Albert – war-weary. And this summer we've 'ad nowt but rain. Worst summer I've ever known.'

'Aye,' said Albert. 'At this rate we'll be lookin' forward to a bit o' drier weather in the winter.'

The rain was depressing Ida Barlow too.

She sat in her front parlour patching some of Kenneth's clothes while Bessie cut out a pattern on the table. They had made a small profit from their make-do-and-mend activity. Few women wanted to join them but many happily left their mending and alterations to be done. Ida kept her share of the profits in an old teapot and took pleasure in how proud Frank would be when he came home to find a little nest-egg.

David was having an afternoon nap, Kenneth had just gone back to school after his lunch and she and Bessie had just eaten beetroot sandwiches followed by a cake made with dried eggs and a bit of lard. 'I'm fed up with eatin' animal innards,' said Ida, out of the blue. 'I've tried 'em now – sweetbreads, chitterlin's, tripe, kidneys and liver. There's nowt could make me eat 'earts and brains.'

Bessie, scissors poised, said, 'Reminds me of the depression years and they was a treat then.'

'Well, I don't know where the butcher gets 'em all from,' said Ida. 'He's never got any good cuts left but he'll always say, "I've got some lovely offal, love."'

'A nice stuffed slow-roasted 'eart is what Albert likes. A few vegetables with that and it goes down a treat.'

Ida began to feel slightly queasy and wanted to change the subject. 'It's the poor kids I feel sorry for.'

'Eatin' offal?'

'No,' said Ida, smiling at long last. 'This bloomin' rain. Kenneth 'ates the rain and 'e 'asn't been out to play with Billy Walker for ages. For some reason Annie's stopped him playing with Kenneth.'

''E's 'ad a very short 'aircut, that Billy,' said Bessie, as she paused for a long faultless cut through the cloth. 'I reckon 'e's got nits. I bet Annie Walker's blamin' everyone and keepin' him away from other kiddies.'

Ida began scratching her head immediately. 'I'd better check my two,' she said. 'You'd think we 'ad enough to worry about without nits, wouldn't you?'

'Aye, pet, but things could be worse,' said Bessie. 'At least 'Itler's gettin' his comeuppance now.'

''E doesn't 'ave to eat offal though, does 'e?'

''E's a vegetarian,' said Bessie.

''E never is.'

'My Albert told me. 'E knows ever such a lot. So you stop frettin', Ida dear, 'cos 'Itler will be eating nowt but 'umble pie soon.'

226

Ena Sharples waited up for her showdown with Vera but she fell asleep and it had to wait until morning. It was only six a.m. and Vera was hardly awake.

'What this I 'ear, my girl?' demanded Ena.

Vera, trying to wash her face at the sink, mumbled under the towel. 'About what, Mam?'

'Don't you act the innocent wi' me. I know about your weddin' plans.'

'It's Bob's family. They want a church do.'

'Take that towel off your face and look at me.'

Vera did as she was told, sheepishly. 'Sorry,' she mumbled.

'Sorry?' yelled Ena. 'Sorry? You will be sorry, my girl. This Mission has given you an 'ome all these years and now you turn your back on us.'

''Is mam says she won't come to some back-street chapel and they'll pay for everything, so–' Vera broke off, intimidated by Ena's expression.

Ena could feel her chest nearly explode with fury. 'Back-street chapel? How dare she? This chapel has provided shelter for 'undreds. Clean blankets and towels and cups of tea. What's St Mary's ever done?

Nowt, that's what! And you, yer great puddin', couldn't even stand up for yerself. I bet you said, "Yes, Mrs Lomax, no, Mrs Lomax," like a bloomin' parrot.'

'I did try, Mam,' interrupted Vera.

'I did try, Mam,' mimicked Ena. 'You've got no backbone, girl. Sometimes I wonder if I wasn't given the wrong baby at the 'ospital they 'ad to take me to. You were trouble, Vera, even before yer was born.

Vera began to cry and wiped her eyes with a corner of the towel. There was nothing she could say, her mother just wasn't going to listen.

'And you can stop that skrikin', that'll do yer no good. You must get round to the Lomax 'ouse and say you'll 'ave marriage service 'ere.'

Vera looked up, her eyes full of tears. 'No,' she said, in a wavering voice.

'What do yer mean, girl, no?'

'Bob and me 'ave decided and that's an end to it,' said Vera, jutting out her chin defiantly.

Ena had never heard that tone in her daughter's voice before but she guessed Vera would give in in the end. She softened her voice. 'Now look 'ere, Vera. I shall be right proud of you on the day. I can do a nice

228

little tea for you 'ere. It'll be a grand day.'

'No,' said Vera, still defiant. 'It's my day and I'll do as I want.'

'Well, I'll not be comin' to see you wed in a church,' said Ena, her mouth set in grim determination.

'Aye, Mam. Do as yer please.'

Ena opened her mouth but Vera was already slipping on her jacket and walking to the back door. She turned as she put her hand on the latch. 'It's next Saturday, Mam, at two thirty.'

Ena's emotions seesawed between anger, surprise and misery. But it was pride that won the day. 'You'll be on yer own, then,' she said.

Vera left without another word and Ena recognized at long last that Vera was now grown-up and that she had lost control.

For some time Ena sat and prayed. Of one thing she was sure. God was on her side.

CHAPTER FIFTEEN

Summer 1944: Sustained Attacks by V1s Over Southern England

Minnie Caldwell rarely got letters and when one did land on her mat it always made her slightly anxious, especially if she couldn't immediately recognize the handwriting. She'd picked up the letter and stared at the postmark. It was local, but no one in Weatherfield would write to her and her bills always came in plain brown envelopes. This was pure white and now that she realized she couldn't guess the identity of the sender she tore it open. It was from Bessie Street School. Would she please see the headmaster as soon as possible, at her convenience, to discuss a matter relating to Dieter Holliman?

Minnie's first reaction was to take the letter straight to Ena. She'd already slipped her coat on but at the back door she took a deep breath and decided that if Dieter had been misbehaving at school no one else need know about it.

All the way to the school Minnie tried to work out what Dieter might have done. At home he was always well behaved and polite. Had he been fighting or cheeking the teachers? Minnie couldn't believe he would do such things. It was more likely that the others were picking on him.

By the time Minnie was ushered into the office she was as nervous as any child on their first day at school. Mr Barnstable, with his handsome face and kind eyes, instantly put her at her ease.

'Do sit down, Mrs Caldwell,' he said. 'I deliberately didn't mention any reason for wanting to see you about Dieter. First, let me say that he is a credit to the school – he's bright and diligent, polite and attentive, and he gets on well with the other children.' He paused. 'I don't want to worry you, Mrs Caldwell, but it's been reported to me that a man has been asking questions about Dieter.'

'What sort of questions?' asked Minnie anxiously.

Mr Barnstable smiled. 'Please don't be too worried. He hasn't approached Dieter. It seems this man asked another child to point Dieter out and then he stood and watched him in the playground.'

Minnie nibbled her bottom lip. 'Did 'e wear a long black coat?'

'Yes,' Mr Barnstable said. 'You know about him, then?'

Minnie nodded. 'I 'ad 'eard 'e were asking around Weatherfield some time back.'

'I'm sorry to say that I've only just heard about this. It seems he first appeared some weeks back but this visit was just two days ago.'

'Oh dear,' murmured Minnie. 'I think 'e must be someone from the orphanage.'

Mr Barnstable shook his head. 'I rang the orphanage but the new matron knew nothing about Dieter and nothing about the man.'

Minnie fiddled nervously with the handles of her shopping-bag. 'What should I do, then?' she asked.

'All I can suggest at the moment,' said Mr Barnstable, 'is that you collect him from school each day.'

'Aye,' said Minnie, standing up. 'I'll do that.'

Minnie couldn't get away from Bessie Street School fast enough. Now she *did* want to see Ena. She'd know what to do. And she'd have to warn Dieter.

Ena was polishing the Mission chairs when Minnie arrived. 'Well, Minnie, you look as if you've lost sixpence and found a ha'penny.'

'I've bin to Bessie Street School. That bloke's bin watchin' my Dieter.'

'The black-coat man?'

'Aye. 'E's bin round this week.'

'Well, Minnie Caldwell, I'll 'ave to pay another visit to that orphanage, won't I?'

''E's not from there – the headmaster checked.'

Ena sighed. 'Best put kettle on then, and work summat out.'

Ena had always kept a photo of Vera on the mantelpiece in her flat. Minnie noticed it had gone. Since Vera had got married and moved away, Ena hadn't been herself at all. For a while she stopped going into the Rovers and had taken instead to playing the harmonium and singing hymns all on her own. She'd lost weight too.

'Are you all right, Ena?' asked Minnie. 'You 'aven't been quite yerself since your Vera left.'

Ena's eyes sparked. 'Minnie Caldwell, I'd rather you didn't mention that name to me. She's no daughter of mine. I've cast her out.'

233

'But it says in the Bible–' began Minnie.

'Don't you tell me owt about the Bible, Minnie Caldwell. I knows the Bible. "Honour thy father and mother", that's what it says. And she didn't. Now let's talk about lookin' after young Dieter. There's nowt to be gained by talkin' about the cross I 'ave to bear.'

Minnie noticed that Ena had perked up no end at the thought of a new challenge.

'We don't want to frighten 'im away, Minnie,' said Ena, as she measured out the tea-leaves.

'We don't?'

'I've just said we don't. We need to catch 'im red-'anded.'

''Ow will we do that, Ena?'

'We'll tek it in turns to be at Bessie Street School at playtimes and dinnertimes and we'll catch 'im.'

''Ow?'

'What do yer mean, 'ow?'

''E'll run off, won't 'e, Ena? And I can't run and I've never seen you run.'

'I'll 'ave you know, Minnie Caldwell, I won the egg-and-spoon race and the three-legged race when I was at school.'

'That was a long time ago, Ena, and it won't 'elp if 'e puts up a fight.'

'I'll tell you summat,' said Ena. 'We wouldn't be winnin' this war if Winnie were Minnie. You'd throw your 'ands up if one single Nazi did a goose-step down Coronation Street.'

'I would not!'

'That's as mebbe, but you've got to keep your wits about you. We don't know who this bloke is or what 'e wants.'

''E could be a spy,' suggested Minnie.

'I shouldn't think there's owt Dieter could tell 'im.'

'You never know, Ena. 'E did get out of Germany so mebbe this bloke 'as been sent by 'Itler to find out 'ow 'e did it.'

Ena squinted at Minnie. 'Sometimes,' she said, 'you surprise me, Minnie.'

'Why's that, Ena?'

'Because you talk nowt but bloomin' tosh. You know Dieter and 'is mam got out before the war even started. Sometimes I think you're as deaf as yer own mother.'

Elsie Tanner had two letters that morning. She recognized the handwriting on both: one was from Steve, the other from Antonio. She didn't need to waste time choosing which to open first. Steve would always be the winner.

Her hand trembled as she opened the letter and she felt a wave of disappointment at its length and that it had taken three weeks to arrive. He apologized for not writing before, said how much he missed her and that he was thinking about her all the time. He was in France but he couldn't tell her exactly where. His final lines were the best: 'I meant what I said, Elsie. However long it takes I'll be back for you and we'll be married. That's a solemn promise. All my love and kisses, honey, your ever-loving Steve.' She read it again and again and felt a mixture of hope and fear: hope that he meant what he said and fear that either he wouldn't come back or that something or someone would come between them.

Antonio's letter was longer, contained a crisp five-pound note, and he talked about the last time they had made love, how beautiful she was and how he wished his hands could reach out and touch her breasts, and how each night she should place her own hands on her breasts and think of him. 'You silly sod,' she said aloud, but secretly she was delighted that two good-looking men desired her. Surely *one* of them would come back for her when the war was over. She'd heard nothing from Arnold so maybe he hadn't received the letter from Ena Sharples. With any luck he might have decided by now that he couldn't care less about her and the kids.

There was a postscript to Antonio's letter – 'Christmas is coming. Any room at the inn for some mates to stay? I might be lucky and get a bit of leave soon. *Ciao.*'

Elsie hummed to herself as she walked towards Dot's. She and Sally quite often had Dennis and Linda to stay overnight. In fact, every Friday now she took them round and Dot bathed them, gave them cod-liver oil, syrup of figs and Virol. The Virol was the only thing they liked. When they were peaky or just not eating well, she gave them Parrish's Food. It tasted like iron filings but they didn't seem to mind. The wet summer was past now but even without much sun Dennis and Linda had lost that 'air-raid shelter' grey complexion that most children seemed to have.

She'd just reached the back alley when she saw a telegram boy cycle by. The postman was always welcome, the telegram boy never. Someone was just about to get the worst sort of news. He stopped his bike on her side of the road and she was just wondering who it might be when she realised the lad was knocking on *her* door. She ran, as fast as she could– Please don't let it be Steve, please don't let it be Steve, she kept saying to herself. Breathless, she almost snatched the telegram from the boy's hand. She tore it open to read: WE REGRET TO INFORM YOU ABLE SEAMAN EDWARD ROYSTON HAS DIED IN ACTION FROM INJURIES RECEIVED. LETTER AND EFFECTS TO FOLLOW.

'Any reply, missus?' asked the telegram boy.

Elsie shook her head. It had taken her a few seconds to realize that Edward Royston was her Eddie, the lad who'd taken a real shine to her and her to him, although on her part she'd known he was just passing by and that he'd been too young for her. Poor Eddie, she thought, but why had *she* got the telegram? They were usually sent only to the next of kin.

Dot was coming towards her. 'Where the 'ell 'ave you been? We'll be late for work.'

'I 'ad a telegram.'

'Oh Gawd,' said Dot. 'Who's copped it?'

'That Eddie.'

'That fair-'aired lad who couldn't tek his

eyes off you?'

''E must 'ave put me down as 'is next of kin.'

'Poor little beggar,' said Dot. ''E was a 'andsome lad.'

'And a nice fella. I could 'ave fallen for 'im if I'd put me mind to it.'

'Elsie, my old mate,' said Dot, putting an arm around her, 'you could fall for a gorilla if 'e was good to you.'

'That's not true. I'm quite fussy.'

'Aye,' laughed Dot. 'Two gins, and to you all men look like Clark Gable.'

They walked to Elliston's, and Elsie told Dot about the letters from Steve and Antonio. 'I've got me doubts about that Antonio,' said Elsie thoughtfully.

'Why's that, then? Do you think 'e's in the Mafia?'

''Is letter was postmarked Manchester. Now, if 'e's in the country why 'asn't 'e bin to see me lately?'

'Mebbe he got a mate to post it for 'im.'

Elsie thought about that. It did seem a possibility. He had lots of mates. ''E did send me a fiver, Dot, so I'll treat you tonight – nice fish supper and a few drinks at the Rovers.'

Dot smiled. ''E might be a bit of a mystery

man, Elsie, but 'e is good to yer.'

Elsie had to agree with that, but when she got to work she found the only person she thought about was Eddie. He was the sort of bloke who would have given her the moon. He'd been just nineteen. At least he'd found his manhood with her. He had deserved that at the very least.

Ena had made a list of 'school watchers' so that no one was overburdened with the task. Albert Tatlock, Bessie and even Tom Hewitt and Ida Barlow were on the team. Day after day they kept watch on the school playground, but there was no sign of the man in the black coat.

'It's bin three weeks now, Ena,' said Martha when they met in the Snug of the Rovers on Friday night. 'Don't you think it's time to pack it up?'

Ena sipped her milk stout thoughtfully. ''Ow long 'as this war been goin' on, Martha Longhurst?'

'Five years.'

'Doesn't that tell yer somethin'?'

Minnie, who was sitting quietly watching the other customers, said, 'We are winnin' the war, aren't we, Ena?'

'Who asked you, Minnie?' said Ena

crossly. 'I was talkin' to Martha. And of course we're winnin' the war. Don't you know owt?'

'I only 'eard,' said Minnie undeterred, 'that 'Itler's new rockets, them V1s are killin' 'undreds in London. 'E could win the war with them. They don't 'ave pilots, do they?'

Ena gave Minnie her sternest look. 'I can see you've bin readin' your squares of newspaper in the privy again.'

'I 'ave not,' said Minnie. 'I 'eard it from Albert Tatlock and 'e 'eard it from the wireless.'

'Well, 'e's no business filling your 'ead with doom and gloom. There's enough of that round 'ere without 'im spreadin' all them Lord Haw-Haw lies.'

'Mebbe Lord Haw-Haw's right,' said Minnie, with a touch of defiance.

Ena leaned forward. 'Minnie Caldwell, if you was a German you'd be taken out and shot if you talked owt about defeat.'

Minnie frowned. 'But I'm not a German.'

Ena shook her head despairingly. 'Talkin' to you, Minnie, is as 'ard as rubbin' two wet sticks together to mek fire. Now, are we goin' to talk about your Dieter or not?'

'Yes, Ena.'

''Bout time. Any road – scare stories or not – we carry on. This bloke may know we're watchin' school and 'e may just 'ave to tek a chance one day.'

'Chance for what, Ena?' asked Martha.

'A chance to snatch Dieter away.'

'Why would 'e want to do that?' asked Martha.

''Ow the 'eck would I know?' said Ena irritably. 'Mebbe, 'is family's important or summat.'

'Mebbe 'e's a prince,' suggested Minnie.

''E may be a prince to you, Minnie Caldwell, but I don't think Germans 'ave princes, do they?'

Neither Minnie nor Martha had an answer to that.

'So it's decided, then. We all agree,' said Ena. 'We keep watch on the school.'

'If you say so, Ena,' said Minnie.

'Aye,' murmured Martha.

It was two days later that the parcel was delivered to No. 11. Elsie thought at first that it was from Antonio but when she tore off the brown paper and saw inside she realized it was not. There was a letter, a wristwatch, a fountain pen, a penknife, a compass and a Bible – she recognized the watch as Eddie's. Seeing his few possessions laid out before her on the table made her legs feel wobbly. She sat down to read the letter:

Dear Mrs Tanner,
My name is Daphne Harold and I am a Navy nurse. Eddie was not well enough to write this letter himself so he has dictated it to me. As you probably know by now, he designated you his next of kin so by now you have his effects. Sadly Eddie died of his wounds a few days ago. He was very brave and he did so want you to have this last letter. These are his own words and they do show how much his stay with you meant to him. May I offer my sincere condolences.

Hello Elsie,
Nursie here is writing down everything I say. I'm being well looked after and I'm not in any pain but I've well and truly copped it.
    I think about you all the time. I know you thought I was a bit young for you but I was very old in my head. The stay I had at your place was the best time I've ever had. I can't remember any family – my mam abandoned me. Just having a place to go for my leave was smashing and you were so good to me.

243

You gave me the best night of my life and I don't think I'd be dying so happy if I hadn't met you. I hope little Linda and Dennis are well. I've enclosed my life savings inside my Bible. It's not much but I hope you treat yourself and the kids.

I do hope you'll say a prayer for me. Perhaps one day we'll meet up on the other side. All my love, Eddie.

Elsie opened the Bible and took out the four five-pound notes. Then she burst into tears. Not only had a lovely lad died but he might have been a man who could have loved her just for herself, the man who, in bleak moments, she doubted she would ever find. 'God bless you, Eddie love,' she whispered, as she slipped on his wristwatch. I'll never forget you, she thought, not as long as I live.

CHAPTER SIXTEEN

Winter 1944:V2 Kills 271 in Rex Cinema

Ida Barlow had begun sorting out her box of Christmas decorations in late November. All she needed now was the tree, some crêpe paper and paper chains. She'd saved some dried fruit and sugar and she had a tin of ham and another of salmon put by. Bessie had given her two jars of mincemeat and some bottled fruit, so apart from little presents for Kenneth and David she was organized.

Bessie had called in that morning to suggest they join forces for Christmas dinner.

'We'd love to 'ave you, Ida,' she said. 'Albert's getting a 'uge turkey for his Christmas bonus, I've got sherry and port put by and I know Albert's been whittling away mekkin' wooden toys for your Kenneth and your David.'

Ida gave Bessie a hug. 'We'd love to come – only you must promise me you'll come to us on Boxing Day.'

'Aye, that'll be a treat,' said Bessie. 'Christmas is nowt like the same without kiddies.'

'Your Beattie will be 'ome soon,' said Ida. 'This time next year it will all be over.'

Bessie nodded. 'I do 'ope so. The trouble is our Beattie 'as settled in so well in the country she's all but forgotten us. She's found a new life, see, and we can't offer 'er the same things.'

'You're 'er flesh and blood,' said Ida. 'That's what matters.'

'Aye,' murmured Bessie. 'I 'ope you're right.'

'Your Beattie is like Dieter – in a strange place but quite 'appy and well looked after.'

Bessie smiled. 'Talkin' of the little lad, I thought Minnie might like to join us all for Christmas dinner.'

'That's a nice idea,' said Ida. 'Our Kenneth will 'ave a bit of company – but what about Ena?'

'What about 'er?'

'I think she goes to Minnie's on Christmas Day on account of Minnie's mother.'

'Oh, aye,' said Bessie. 'We'll work summat out.'

When Bessie left, Ida got to work. She was

making Bessie a dress as a Christmas present from some material she'd had left over and forgotten about. There was only just enough and she hadn't got a pattern but she'd sewn up the side seams and all she had to do now was fit the sleeves and hem it. It was as she was putting in the second sleeve she remembered that she hadn't written to Frank for three days. It was even more of a shock to realize that she hadn't even thought about him since she'd last written.

Annie Walker always decorated the Rovers on 1 December. The Christmas tree had to wait until the fourteenth but this year she had Teresa, and Annie had to admit that her help was invaluable. Teresa had already made a Christmas cake and the pudding and was suggesting she would also cook the Christmas dinner. Annie had drawn the line at that.

Her main problem this year was what to do about John. He'd remained persistent and still visited after closing time. Annie couldn't resist him: she had no real friends – couldn't mix with other women in the day and her customers she kept at arm's length. John was a lifeline and he opened up the worlds of books, music and even politics to

her. He promised even more after the war –
a country cottage, trips abroad, visits to the
theatre, an end to the routine of life at the
Rovers. Annie tried to keep alive the
memory of her love for Jack but she hadn't
even had a letter for weeks and his last visit
had been an unmitigated disaster. She
didn't want to admit it but Jack was fast
becoming someone in the past, someone for
whom she felt fondness but nothing more. It
was John now who stirred her physically and
mentally. With him she could be the person
she wanted to be. Mrs John Barnstable,
headmaster's wife, she thought, was far
more her natural self than Mrs Jack Walker,
publican's wife.

She had already bought and wrapped
Christmas presents for Billy and Joan. Their
stockings would contain an orange, a few
sweets, some Plasticine for Billy and a small
doll for Joan. What to buy John was a
problem, but she'd finally decided on cuff-
links and a Thomas Hardy book. She hadn't
forgotten Teresa either: she'd bought her a
new Bible, some soap and a tin of talcum
powder.

All things considered, Annie was looking
forward to Christmas. She hoped that
Teresa would want time off but she hadn't

broached the subject yet. Her talk of cooking Christmas dinner had come as a surprise. The idea of John sitting down on Christmas Day with Teresa there wasn't what Annie had in mind. Would he want to bring his mother along too? Maybe it would be a case of the more the merrier, but Annie wasn't convinced. She would have preferred Christmas dinner with John as the only guest.

Elsie Tanner looked at her front room and wagged a finger at the three servicemen who had descended on her a few days before Christmas. One had ebony skin and the best physique she'd ever seen – his name was Tyrone Kingston and he sang gospel songs in a voice as rich as the black treacle, or molasses, as he called it, that he liked on his porridge. He was in the American Army and recovering from injuries received in the Normandy landings. The other two, Norman Jenkins and 'Chalky' White, were both sailors with nowhere else to go. They seemed puny compared with the massive Tyrone, yet they were more aggressive, always arguing among themselves, and they were untidy.

'Now, look 'ere, lads,' said Elsie, trying to

sound stern, 'I've got things to do and I can't do 'em with you lot sprawled all over me floor.'

Chalky, who had been listening to the radio lying on his back by the fire, struggled to his feet. 'Shall we go down the pub, Elsie?'

'Aye,' she said, 'that's a good idea. And don't come back till closing.'

'I'll go with them, ma'am,' said Tyrone. 'Keep an eye on them.'

As they were leaving Tyrone said, 'If you like, ma'am, I'll cook supper for you tonight.'

Elsie laughed. 'That's the best offer I've 'ad in a long time. I'd invite Dot and Sally but I've done nowt about doin' any messages.'

'Messages?' he queried.

'Larder's empty,' said Elsie. 'I haven't 'ad time to join the ruddy queues.'

'You leave the provisions to me, ma'am. I know where to go.'

Her guests had left at midday. By seven there was no sign of them. At seven thirty she'd put Dennis and Linda to bed after she'd given them Bovril sandwiches and hot milk, and once she was sure they were asleep she crept out of the house to buy herself a fish supper. On the way back she peeped into the Rovers, not only to see if they were there but to have a drink. She was about to approach the bar when she saw Len Fairclough drinking on his own. She wasn't sure if he'd seen her but she made a hasty exit, nearly tripping over in her high heels in the process. She'd only gone a few yards when she heard footsteps behind her.

'Elsie, 'ang on a tick.'

She turned to see Len's face looming towards her in the darkness. ''Ello, Len. You back on leave again?'

'I only lasted a few weeks – me leg played up. They 'ad to reset it and I'm in plaster again.'

'Look on the bright side, Len. At this rate you could still be 'ere when the war ends.'

'I'd rather be back at sea – I 'ate 'anging about wi' nothing to do.'

Elsie looked at her watch. 'Any road, I can't stop to chat – I've left the kids asleep in bed.'

'No need to be sarky wi' me,' he said with a grin. 'I'll walk you 'ome.'

'I 'ad to 'ave a look in Rovers to see if my lodgers were there,' she explained. 'They went out at dinnertime and I 'aven't seen them since.'

'What do you expect?' he said, falling into step beside her. 'They'll be drinkin' Weatherfield dry.'

'They're good lads,' said Elsie. 'One of 'em was goin' to cook for me tonight but I was starvin' so I've bin down the chippy.'

'I can smell 'em.'

'You can 'ave some,' said Elsie, 'so as you know I don't bear you any grudge.'

Elsie didn't bother with plates, just shared out the fish and chips in the newspaper it had been wrapped in and added extra salt and vinegar. She handed Len his parcel. 'If they come back steamin' drunk,' he said, 'and you can't 'andle 'em, Elsie, you get round to my place and I'll sort it out for you.'

'I'll manage 'em, Len. They'll only want to sleep it off.'

'Elsie?'

'What?'

'I do care what 'appens to you, you know.'

'I know you do, Len – you're a good mate.'

Len looked uncomfortable and rubbed his hands nervously. 'I want to be more than just a mate.'

'What do you mean, Len?'

'Do I 'ave to spell it out? Don't act like you're no sharper than an 'orse's bum.'

'There's no need to raise your voice to me, Len Fairclough.'

'You'd know it if I raised me voice.'

Elsie stood up from the table and crumpled up the remains of the paper from their fish supper. Then she smiled and threw the balls of paper at him. 'You don't frighten me, Len Fairclough.'

'I don't want to frighten you, Elsie – I want to woo you.'

'Don't talk so daft, Len. Mates is mates. Anyway, if you and I got together you'd want me to be respectable. And I don't want to be respectable. I want to 'ave fun. You'd want slippers by the fire, a home-made pie in the oven, and me darnin' ruddy socks as I listened to Arthur Askey on the radio.'

'That sounds all right to me,' said Len. 'What more could a man ask?'

'See, Len, that's just my point. That's what a lot of men want–'

'Most men,' he interrupted.

'Aye, and most women want summat different. Look at the girls round 'ere – the married ones with their 'usbands away. They may work 'ard and not 'ave much money but they've made their own fun, found new friends. The men will come back, the women will lose their jobs and they'll be

253

lucky to get a shandy on a Saturday night once a month.'

Len looked at her thoughtfully. 'You sound as if you don't want the war to end.'

'Mebbe I don't,' murmured Elsie. 'Even if Arnold came back a changed man I wouldn't want 'im. I know now there's men who know 'ow to treat a woman.'

'I suppose you're sayin' I'm not one of 'em.'

Elsie patted Len's cheek. 'There's no need to look like that. There's a girl for you somewhere – even with your gammy leg.'

Len stared at her for a moment. Then he said, with a grin, 'You know 'ow to butter up a bloke, don't you? My leg won't be in plaster for ever, then I'll come chasin' yer. You're the only one for me, Elsie Tanner, and one day you'll realize it.'

When he'd gone Elsie lit a cigarette and stared into the fire. Len was a decent bloke, hard-working, reliable, and he had a sense of humour, but underneath all that she sensed he wanted to control her. The thought that he might be a man who *could* was what frightened her.

Elsie dragged another chair across the room and rested her feet on that. She slipped her coat over her shoulders as she noticed the fire was nearly out, smoked one more Player's and fell asleep.

She woke up at the sound of the back door opening. 'About ruddy time,' she said without opening her eyes. She waited for sounds of drunken revelling but there was only a shuffling and a faint groaning noise. Her eyes sprang open and there stood Chalky blood dribbling from his mouth, one eye half closed, supporting Norman, who was covered in mud and blood, had a bleeding nose and a large swelling on his forehead.

'What the 'eck's 'appened?' she said, springing up to help Chalky support Norman and guide him to a chair.

'We was set on,' said Chalky, wiping the blood from his mouth with the back of his hand.

'Where's Tyrone?' asked Elsie.

Chalky looked at Norman, who looked away sheepishly. 'We did our best, Elsie, honest we did. There was too many of them. They chased us down by the canal.'

'What the 'ell's 'appened to Tyrone?' demanded Elsie.

Norman, whose eyes were beginning to close, peered through the slits to say, 'We lost 'im.'

''Ow could yer lose 'im?' yelled Elsie. ''E's six foot four and built like a tank.'

'We've bin looking but it's pitch dark out there,' said Norman. 'It was 'im they were after. We took 'em on but there was too many of 'em. We 'ad to do a runner and we thought Ty was behind us but 'e wasn't.'

'Did you go back to look?'

'Aye, but there was no sign of 'im.'

Elsie grabbed her coat and a torch. 'You two clean yourselves up and get to bed. I'll get 'elp and go and find 'im.' As she went to the back door she said, 'I'll talk to you two in the morning. At this rate you won't survive till bloomin' Christmas.'

As she rushed along to Len's she realized that some paying guests were more like schoolboys and she was sounding like their headmistress. She banged loudly on Len's front door, not caring who she woke up in the Street. 'Len, wake up, I need your 'elp,' she shouted.

He came to the door with his one good leg in his trousers the other trouser leg at half mast over his plaster. 'Do you want to wake the whole bloody Street, Elsie Tanner?'

'It's Tyrone. The lads 'ave been beaten up and Tyrone's missing.'

'Where?'

'By the canal.'

'Right – you knock up Albert Tatlock,' said Len, 'and then go 'ome. We'll find 'im.'

'I'm not goin' 'ome, I'm comin' with you. With your leg you might not be much 'elp.'

'Elsie, don't argue. Just get Albert.'

Elsie had no intention of arguing: she was going with them and that was that. When he answered the door Albert already had his tin helmet on. Elsie waited while he put some clothes on over his pyjamas and wondered if he *ever* took his helmet off.

Len looked daggers at Elsie but said nothing until they got near the canal. Then he said, 'If you fall in, Elsie, I'll do nowt to fish you out.'

The canalside was dark and deserted. It began to rain, and the only sound they could hear was the faint hoot of an owl and rain on the water. They yelled Tyrone's name as they walked and shone their torches back and forth. Elsie was squinting as the rain whipped at her face, but she'd seen something in the water. 'Over there,' she shouted, pointing.

Len hobbled over to investigate. 'Elsie, you stay back,' he called out.

'Oh, Gawd,' Elsie heard him say, followed by, 'What the 'eck?'

'What is it?' she asked, trying to move forward, but with Albert hanging on to her arm trying to pull her back.

Len was limping towards them with a large round object in his hand. 'I thought it was 'is ruddy 'ead,' he said.

Elsie laughed in relief. 'That's a pumpkin. Steve told me about pumpkin pie. Tyrone must be 'ere somewhere. 'E must've been plannin' to cook it.'

Albert, impatient to get out of the rain, walked on ahead. Len and Elsie followed at a slower pace. Elsie's teeth were chattering with cold, and when Len put his arm round her she was grateful for the warmth of his body. They walked on and on. Elsie's shoes were letting in water and as the ground got wetter her heels sank into the mud. She had never walked this far along the canal and she was surprised to see a lock.

Albert saw Tyrone first – he couldn't miss the big man, straddled precariously over the side of the lock gate.

''E's not dead, is 'e?' yelled Elsie.

Albert felt for his pulse. 'His heart's still beatin'. But 'e's out cold.'

Between them they heaved and tugged the huge man on to the ground. ''E's eaten too much pumpkin pie by the weight of 'im,' said Albert, trying to catch his breath. Once they had Tyrone flat on his back he groaned a little. Elsie felt his face: it was icy cold. He'd gone out in a thick black jacket with a fleecy lining; now he wore only his underpants and a vest with his shoes and socks.

'We can't carry 'im back,' said Len.

'We 'ave to keep 'im warm,' said Elsie, taking off her coat and putting it over him. Len knelt down with difficulty and began shaking him and slapping his face. 'Don't 'urt 'im,' said Elsie, pushing Len aside.

'*You* bring 'im round, then, Elsie. He's passed out. I bet a bloke like 'im could drink a barrel of beer on his own. He could be out cold till mornin'.'

'Let's get 'im on 'is feet,' suggested Albert, 'and then you and me, Len, can see if we can drag 'im along.'

'Shall I run and get some 'elp?' asked Elsie.

'No. We'll need you to 'elp us,' said Len.

Albert took off his woollen scarf and tied it round Tyrone's neck. Only one arm would fit into Elsie's coat but it was better than nothing. Then the two men hauled him upright and crouched down to fix his arms over their shoulders. 'One, two, three – *up!*'

called out Albert.

Tyrone's legs dragged lifelessly along as they began the slow walk home, and Len's leg hurt under the strain. He hoped he'd make it back to Elsie's house without doing even more damage to it. Soaked to the skin and struggling to walk, Elsie took off her shoes and stuffed one into each of Len's jacket pockets.

Half-way home, both Len and Albert were exhausted and had to pause for a breather.

'I'll take over for a bit, Len,' said Elsie. 'You want to watch out for that leg.'

'Don't fuss, Elsie,' Len said. 'I just need a bit of a rest. Why don't you take over from Albert for a bit?'

'Will you let me, Mr Tatlock?'

Albert looked uncertain. 'If you're sure you can manage.'

'It'll keep me warm,' she said.

'Aye,' he said. 'It'll do that all right.'

The sheer weight of Tyrone came as a shock to Elsie and she felt as if her whole body was being pressed into the ground. After a few yards she felt exhausted. Then, through the rain, she saw torchlight and shapes. 'It's the ruddy cavalry,' shouted Len. Elsie couldn't speak – she had no breath left.

The 'cavalry' came in the form of Chalky and Norman. Only an hour or so earlier they had been near to collapse. Now they had revived, and although they could hardly see through their swollen eyes they took Tyrone from Elsie and Len, who leaned his arm across Elsie's shoulders, 'To take the weight off me leg,' he said, and winked at her mischievously.

When they reached No. 11 they managed somehow to get Tyrone up the stairs and on to the bed. Elsie gave him a brisk rub with a towel, which made him groan. She took that to be a good sign. When he felt warmer Elsie went downstairs to read the Riot Act. ''Ow could you let 'im get in that state?' she stormed. ''Ow ever much did 'e drink?'

Len was making tea, Albert had gone home, and Chalky and Norman had stripped off and were rubbing themselves down with towels. Chalky started to answer but Len interrupted, 'You tek them wet clothes off, Elsie, or you'll catch your death.'

For once Elsie agreed. 'I'm near perished but not as bad as poor Tyrone. Why didn't you two keep an eye out for 'im?'

'We did, Elsie,' said Chalky. 'It wasn't–'

'Elsie, get that wet kit off,' interrupted Len.

'Aye-aye, Captain,' said Elsie, giving him a mock salute.

When she came downstairs again, Chalky and Norman, wearing towels, were fast asleep and snoring.

'You've got to give this lark up,' said Len. 'You'll get a reputation you'll never live down.'

'Good,' said Elsie. 'I don't give a damn what people round 'ere think of me.'

'I'm warnin' you, Elsie. It'll all backfire on you. I know you've been skivin' off work, sayin' you're poorly. Elliston's will only put up with so much. You'll lose your job, and then 'ow will you feed the kids?'

'My kids won't ruddy starve. I'll feed 'em 'owever I 'ave to get the money.'

Len picked up his wet coat. 'One day, Elsie, you'll be standin' on a street corner, with a short skirt and a freezin' bum. You'll still be young but you'll look old, and you'll wonder why you didn't listen to me.'

'Bugger off, Len.'

'I'm goin', but think on, Elsie. That Eyetie of yours isn't all he seems.'

'What do you mean by that?' she asked, hands on hips, more than ready now for a scrap.

'You'll tek no notice of what I say, Elsie,

you're too bloody stubborn. You'll find out.'

Before she could answer Len walked out. 'Well, bugger you, Len Fairclough,' she shouted after him. 'I don't need 'elp from anyone – or your bloody advice.'

In the armchair Chalky opened one eye and said, 'What's up?'

'You can shut your trap too, Chalky White. I've just about 'ad enough for one day.'

CHAPTER SEVENTEEN

Christmas Eve 1944: V2 Rockets Bomb Manchester. Hundreds Killed

Ena Sharples wasn't best pleased that Minnie Caldwell was going to Bessie Tatlock's for her Christmas dinner. Ena had hoped to hear from Vera, but although she'd sent her daughter a Christmas card she hadn't had one in return.

Minnie had seemed excited at the thought of spending Christmas surrounded by children. Ena had taken round a pot plant, a colouring book and some crayons for Dieter, but although Minnie gave her tea and cake, Ena could see she was getting in the way of the marathon bake of mince-pies. As usual, Minnie had been apprehensive: 'The Germans won't mek war at Christmas, will they, Ena?' she'd asked. 'I mean they did 'ave a sing-song in the trenches in the first war.'

'They 'ad a bit of lull over Christmas one year,' said Ena, 'but they didn't 'ave 'Itler then, did they? And this war is nowt like the first one.'

'Aye,' said Minnie. ''Fore I forget, I 'ad a message for you from Martha. She says she wants you to 'ave your dinner with 'er.'

'Oh she does, does she? Well, you tell 'er I'll be with our Vera.'

'Will you, Ena? That'll be nice.'

That Martha's invitation had come the day before Christmas Eve, forcing Ena to tell a fib, irritated her but Ena wasn't going to have any one feel sorry for *her*. She did say sorry to God in her prayers but she was convinced He knew that some little white lies were justified.

Today was Christmas Eve and there was a midnight service, so Ena planned to do a bit of baking herself. She wasn't going to let Minnie's mince-pies outshine what she could provide, and she reasoned that she'd have more worshippers if she could provide a bit of a spread after the service.

As for tomorrow, she'd bought a scrawny little chicken and Minnie had given her a Christmas pudding, so she wouldn't starve. But she knew that after the Christmas Day service at eleven o'clock she wouldn't see a soul. Even the Rovers closed on the evening of Christmas Day.

It was still early but Mrs Foyle's Corner Shop opened at five thirty for the news-papers so Ena decided to be first in the queue for whatever was going. She'd heard a rumour that some chocolate might be off ration for a few days but she'd heard things like that before and been disappointed.

Ena was also disappointed at the size of the queue. A fine drizzle had set in, umbrellas were up and word was soon passed down the queue that there was plenty of bread but no chocolate. 'That just about sums up this war,' said a grey-haired woman standing in front of her. 'Plenty o' bread and scrape, but nowt tasty like a bit o' chocolate.'

'You should be grateful to 'ave what we do,' said Ena, unable to resist a little ponti-ficating. 'You're old enough to remember the Depression years. This isn't owt like as bad.'

'Who asked you? I wasn't speaking to you, you nosy old bag.'

Ena would have replied, but as the woman turned to her she realized she was much younger than she thought, barely twenty-eight. And now Ena remembered that she came from Kitchener Street. Her name was Alice Fallows: her husband had been on leave and he'd died in his sleep on his first night home. The doctor said it was a heart-attack. A day later Alice's hair had gone grey. Ena decided to put Alice Fallows on her prayer list.

Tyrone had made steady progress and was easy to look after. He hadn't ventured out since being found at the lock. 'I'm not a coward, ma'am,' he'd told her the next day, as they sat having breakfast. Elsie had her usual three cigarettes and three cups of tea. She was on the third when Tyrone explained what had happened. 'I only asked a girl if she'd like a drink and next minute two guys were calling me names – buck nigger and worse. I wasn't planing to get sore about it and I guess I hoped I wouldn't have to fight them, but suddenly there were six of them swearing and blaspheming, and Chalky and Norman waded in and all hell broke loose.'

'Were you drunk, pet?' asked Elsie, who had a soft spot for him. His only fault, as far as she could see, was that he wanted four sugars in his Camp coffee and she was fast running out of sugar.

'No, ma'am. I've signed the pledge. I've never drunk alcohol.'

'So then what happened?'

'We fought, ma'am, and we fought good, but others joined in against us and Chalky said, "Let's make a run for it," but I was slow and they caught up with me. I don't remember being by the canal.'

'Tyrone, you're lucky to be alive.' She touched his huge biceps. 'Must be all that muscle.'

'I owe you, ma'am.'

'Just call me Elsie, for Gawd's sake.'

'Yes, ma'am, Elsie. And I still owe you some of my cooking. Allow me to buy a turkey and cook it US of A style.'

Now it *was* Christmas Eve and Elsie had the biggest turkey she'd ever seen and a man who insisted he was cooking the whole meal. Elsie just knew she and the kids were going to have a good Christmas. Nothing could go wrong now.

It was just after midday when the siren wailed. Elsie shrugged her shoulders. Hitler's army was in retreat everywhere. It was just a false alarm.

Twenty minutes later they heard bombers overhead. 'Hey, ma'am,' said Tyrone, 'don't you think we should get to a shelter?'

'On Christmas Eve?' exclaimed Elsie. 'Mince-pies are in the oven all over Weather-field. I don't know of anyone who won't just tek a chance.'

Tyrone went out on the front step and saw the tail end of dozens of bombers. 'Jeez,' he murmured. 'And we're supposed to be winning.'

He'd just closed the front door when they heard the noise – a great roaring sound as if a locomotive had passed through Coronation Street. Then another and another. Elsie had snatched up the screaming Dennis and Linda. Tyrone threw his arms round all three of them and Chalky White lived up to his name.

Elsie knew this was no ordinary bombing raid. They'd heard Manchester being bombed many times. This was different and the noise was terrifying.

'They're V2s,' shouted Tyrone, above the roaring. 'Come on, let's get out of here.'

It seemed that all the occupants of Coronation Street were on the move at once. Women just picked up their children and ran without coats towards the Mission Hall. Elsie was amazed to see Annie Walker running, with Joan in her arms, closely followed by Teresa. 'Billy!' Annie was calling frantically, 'Billy, answer me.' She was grabbing anyone she saw, saying, 'Have you seen Billy?' Most people were shrugging her off. Elsie noticed, so she handed her two to Tyrone. 'Take 'em to the Mission, please, love.'

'Anything you say, ma'am. I'll take good care of them.' He sang quietly as he ambled off, and both children stopped screaming to listen.

'Where did you last see 'im?' asked Elsie, taking hold of Annie's arm to stop her running round like a headless chicken. Annie turned to Teresa and the girl muttered tearfully, 'He was just outside the back playing with a whip and top and I looked again about two minutes later and he'd gone.'

'There's nowt you can do 'ere. You get to the Mission,' said Elsie. 'I'll get the lads to look for 'im.'

Another huge explosion silenced them and in the distance they could see a pall of black smoke rising. Annie Walker seemed rooted to the spot and Elsie tried to push her along, to no avail. Minnie Caldwell rushed up, her bottom lip trembling. ''Ave you seen my Dieter? 'E went out 'alf an hour ago and I 'aven't seen 'im since.'

Elsie didn't have time to answer as a bomber came into view and someone shouted, 'Down!' They all flung themselves to the ground. The bomber seemed to slow overhead and begin a silent descent. Acrid smoke from the rear of the plane filled the air. This is it, thought Elsie. We've all 'ad it. The deafening noise that followed seemed to confirm that, but then a shout went up – 'It's 'it the Red Rec.' Everyone struggled to their feet and began to run in that direction.

By the time Elsie and everyone else arrived the plane's cockpit was on fire, the fuselage was in pieces and the tail plane had smashed down several potting sheds. Albert Tatlock was shouting for people to get back but everyone stood watching the inferno in dumb horror and fascination. The sound of fire engines joined with the crackling noise of the burning plane, and the sound of collapsing sheds.

A few members of the ARP were pushing people back behind the gates. 'Look at that,' shouted someone. 'Near the cockpit. It's the pilot.' Now the smoke had lifted they could make out the shape of a man crawling away. Elsie was inside the Red Rec when, above all the noise, she heard a cry. At first she thought it was the pilot moaning, but then realized as she ran nearer to him that he was making no sound. He was hideously burnt. She looked down at him and, even though

271

his face was badly burnt, she could see he was very young, only a boy. He said one word: '*Mutter.*'

Albert Tatlock knelt down to him, then got up and pulled her away. "E's dead, Elsie. We can't do anything for 'im.'

'The poor little sod said *"Mutter"*, Mr Tatlock. What does that mean?'

Albert sighed. 'He was asking for his mother, Elsie.'

The fire brigade arrived and word soon spread that people had been killed and many injured in Manchester. Above the noise Elsie again heard a cry. 'Shush,' she yelled. 'There's two kids missing and I can 'ear somethin'.' Suddenly there was a collective silence and, apart from water sizzling on hot metal, nothing.

As the all-clear sounded it seemed the entire population of Weatherfield converged on the Red Rec. Norman and Chalky and Len Fairclough were among them. Tyrone appeared with the children and a distressed Annie Walker. Once Ena Sharples appeared on the scene, however, she tried to take charge. 'I don't know what you're all gawpin' at,' she shouted. 'You should all go 'ome and let the professionals get on with the job.'

'You 'aven't 'eard, then, that little Dieter and Billy Walker are missin', 'ave you?' said Elsie.

'I did 'ear, but they're not 'ere on the Red Rec, are they?' she said, glancing at the chaos and confusion all around. 'It's like ruddy Armageddon,' she muttered.

Elsie didn't know Armageddon from Blackpool but she was worried. 'I thought I 'eard cryin' a few minutes ago.'

Ena's face took on a determined look. 'Well, that's different – why is no one doin' owt?'

One of the firemen stomped towards them. 'You can't 'ang around 'ere. We don't think 'e was carryin' a rocket 'cos you silly beggars would 'ave been blown to kingdom come if 'e had.'

'There's two kiddies missing and there's been cryin' 'eard somewhere round 'ere,' said Ena. The fireman looked across the expanse of smouldering wreckage and at the sheds in varying stages of collapse. 'The crew's busy, so you'll 'ave to get a few men to form a search party.' Then he added, 'And I'm moving out all the women and children – they'll catch their deaths.'

Ida Barlow put an arm around a weeping Annie Walker and led her away.

273

All the men who owned sheds and plots tried to identify their own bits of debris. Elsie saw that some had tears in their eyes. The loss of their land and produce was a big blow. The allotments were their pride and joy. Albert Tatlock's was in the park but he was upset for Tom Hewitt and the other men. Ena, who had no intention of leaving with the other women, said, 'Don't just stand there like a couple of pansies, Tom and Albert. Look for them kiddies. You can always grow more bloomin' sprouts.'

Still-standing shed walls were torn down, tools placed in piles, rubble and peat shifted but there was no sign of the boys. Elsie began to think she'd imagined the cry because since that second sound she'd heard nothing. Then, to her relief, Len Fairclough shouted, 'Quiet! I 'eard something.' Everyone stopped talking and listened but now the dark clouds that had been hidden by smoke opened up and the rain came down in torrents.

The search continued and then suddenly came a weak 'Help. We're down here. Help!'

The voice came from somewhere beneath the ground and everyone crouched down low. Len called out, 'Hang on, lad. Keep shoutin'.'

It was a few minutes later as Len was hobbling across the flooring base of a shed with no sides that he heard another weak 'Help!'

He began lifting the loose boards and there, wedged together, were the dirt-covered faces of Dieter and Billy. Everyone gathered round to see Len try to ease out Billy's head. But it wasn't easy. Billy tried to speak but began to cry instead. His head was firmly stuck. 'We'll have to dig 'em out,' Len said. Albert immediately grabbed a spade. 'With our bare 'ands,' added Len. 'We might 'urt 'em usin' a spade and they might sink further down.'

The earth was soft and damp and both boys whimpered in fear. 'Somebody sing to 'em,' suggested Tom Hewitt. Tyrone, who was digging alongside Len, began singing 'Jingle Bells' in his deep bass voice, and after two choruses Len shouted in triumph. 'Billy's comin' out.' In seconds he was free, closely followed by Dieter. Both boys were wrapped in bits of old sacking and Len and Tyrone couldn't resist hoisting them in the air in triumph. A loud cheer went up.

'Praise the Lord,' said Ena. 'Someone run and tell Annie Walker and Minnie they're safe.'

It was a tired, wet, exhausted group that began walking out of the Red Rec. Billy Walker fell asleep in Len's arms and Dieter explained tearfully to Tyrone, 'We were digging our own shelter. When we heard all the noise we jumped in the hole and covered it up with the planks of wood but then we couldn't get out.'

They'd just reached the gates when a man in a long black coat approached Tyrone. Ena Sharples ran forward instantly and grabbed his arm. 'Caught you!' she cried. 'You've got a bloomin' cheek, comin' 'ere again.'

'You do not understand,' he said.

'Aye,' said Ena. 'But the police will.'

CHAPTER EIGHTEEN

Christmas Day 1944

Annie Walker's Christmas wasn't one she'd ever forget. Billy had been subdued after his rescue but unhurt, and after food and drink he'd fallen asleep clutching his teddy bear.

The Rovers had been full on Christmas Eve, from opening until Annie was forced to eject the last stragglers. By midnight she was still clearing up and putting the bar money into the safe. She felt exhausted and was longing for her bed. Her one last job was to fill Billy and Joan's stockings, then she could finally get off. She was just locking up when she heard a noise outside. Her heart sank. If that was John she would just have to send him away. She unlocked the back door and looked outside. The yard was empty, apart from some barrels and crates. She told herself she was imagining things when suddenly from behind a barrel she caught a glimpse of red. 'Who's there?' she called. 'Come on out.' She advanced towards the barrels. Just as she got there Father Christmas popped up, complete with a long white beard, red coat and white cuffs. She jumped back in surprise. 'John, what are you playing at? You frightened me half to death.'

'John?'

'John?' she repeated uneasily.

'It's Jack,' came a cold voice she hardly recognized. 'So it *is* true.'

'Jack, why didn't you tell me?' she said, in a voice hardly above a whisper. She wished the ground would swallow her up. If he replied, she didn't hear. Her knees felt week, her head was spinning. Father Christmas was ripping off his beard. He was not full of Christmas cheer.

Betty Preston was first up on Christmas morning, not that anyone would have known it was Christmas. There was no tree, no paper chains and the three cards they had received Harold had torn up. 'Jesus Christ never 'ad paper chains 'anging in his stable and I'll 'ave none in mine,' he'd said.

Betty stayed at home purely for love of her mother but she'd had to make her own strategies for coping. One was to use a box number for Ted's letters, another was to go out as much as possible.

She'd slept badly: the rocket attack on the Manchester area and the plane crashing had really frightened her. 'God will protect us,' Harold had said, refusing to let Margaret leave the house. Her mother had wept, saying it wasn't fair that her daughters were placing their lives at risk. 'I *want* to go to a shelter,' Margaret said. 'I'd be fine if Betty 'elps me and steadies me a bit.'

'If you fell,' said Harold cruelly, 'who could pick you up?'

And so it was settled. During the V2 raid Betty and Maggie had clung to their weeping mother and Harold had knelt and prayed. For the first time in her life Betty faced up to the fact that her father wasn't just domineering, overbearing and a religious zealot. He was mad – a madman who had deliberately fattened up his own wife so that she could never leave him.

Margaret had been so upset by the raid that she had refused to go to bed, saying she would rather die sitting upright. Now she sat pale and puffy, covered with crocheted blankets. Her eyes were closed but Betty knew she wasn't asleep. She filled the kettle and lit a taper to fire the gas ring. Nothing happened. 'Mam, there's no gas,' she called.

'The fire's nearly out too,' Margaret called back.

Betty set to straight away, raking out the embers then pulling out the metal ash pan under the grate. It was still fairly hot so she carried it out gingerly to the backyard. There she tipped the embers into the metal dustbin outside that stood next to the pig-bin. Not that the pig-bin ever saw many leftovers in the Preston house. Betty filled a bucket with coal and placed a bundle of wood on top, then struggled back into the house.

'What are we going to do with no gas on Christmas Day?' asked Margaret wearily.

'I don't know,' said Betty. 'I'll get this fire going and when it's nice and 'ot we can put the kettle on top. We could 'ave toast usin' the toastin' fork, and we could roast chestnuts.'

'We can't cook a ten-pound turkey, though, can we?'

'Not unless the gas comes on soon.'

'Your father will go mad,' said Margaret.

Betty raised her eyebrows but said nothing. She arranged the coal and the wood, then she folded some newspaper into strips and wove it between the coals.

Even with a brisk fire the kettle seemed to

take ages to boil and by then Harold and Maggie had appeared. Harold wouldn't believe there was no gas and had to try it for himself. He even tried the gas lamps, but of course they didn't work either.

Suddenly Betty couldn't bear to be in their dark, dreary house any longer. She slipped on her coat and went out. She didn't often cry, but the shock of the raid had upset her and soon tears were welling. All the houses were in darkness and in Coronation Street the only lights she could see were at the Mission. It seemed like an omen and the door was open so she walked inside. There was a small Christmas tree in the entrance and in the chapel area a nativity scene had been placed in one corner. Betty sat down on one of the chairs and cried.

Ena Sharples knew Betty by sight and she knew Harold Preston too. She watched Betty for a while from the back of the Hall then sat down quietly beside her. 'What's up, Betty? It's Christmas Day. You shouldn't be sittin' 'ere skrikin'.'

Betty wiped her face with the back of her hand. 'Gas is off. I think it's off in the whole of Weatherfield.'

'There's no need to break your heart about that, is there?' said Ena, giving her an awkward pat on the back. 'We'll work summat out. Folk will 'ave to do their best with open fires. Or they can find someone who's got electric and we can share the food around – 'ave a party 'ere. Some can bring sandwiches and 'ave their proper Christmas dinners when the gas comes on.'

Betty was silent for a while. She'd never spoken about her family situation to anyone, but now she couldn't stop herself. 'My mam 'asn't left the 'ouse for years, Mrs Sharples.'

'Why's that, then?'

'She's too fat.'

Ena let Betty talk, and the girl told her everything. How her father treated them, how he stuffed Margaret with food and didn't encourage her to do anything for herself, how he kept her in the house during raids. Eventually she stopped.

'I reckon,' said Ena thoughtfully, 'you and your mam and sister need a bit of 'elp from someone. A bit of Christian charity.'

'My dad doesn't believe in charity.'

'I don't mean that sort of charity. Now, dry your eyes, girl, and we'll go and get your mam out of there for the day.'

'She won't come out – 'e won't let 'er.'

Ena smiled grimly. 'Betty, your dad's built

like a string bean. 'Ow's he goin' to stop us? Besides, I've got somethin' to say to 'im.'

Ena led the way back to No. 6 Tile Street. Betty walked slowly behind her, dreading that Ena would make things worse rather than better. Her father wasn't going to let Ena Sharples into the house, of that she was sure.

'You go round the back,' said Ena. 'Tell 'im I'm 'ere and I want words with 'im.'

''E won't come out.'

'You just tell 'im I've got a memory like a bloomin' elephant.'

'Aye. But I know he won't speak to you.'

''E will. You'll see.'

Nervously, Betty gave her father the message, at which he glared furiously. 'What 'ave you bin sayin', girl? She's a terrible evil woman, and you bring 'er to our doorstep – may God forgive you.'

To Betty's great surprise he went to the front door and slammed it shut behind him.

'Well, 'Arold Preston,' said Ena, resting her hand on the doorframe, 'it's a long time since I've seen you.'

'What's all this about, Mrs Sharples? What right 'ave you to interfere with a God-fearin' family?'

'You 'aven't always been God-fearin', 'ave

you, 'Arold?' said Ena slyly.

Harold opened his mouth like a dying fish then closed it again.

'You 'ad trouble findin' yourself a wife, didn't you, 'Arold? Let me think who there was... There was Lily and Cissie and Phyllis. All left you, didn't they? Too much spirit they 'ad. I remember poor Lily best. You was the one who got 'er in the family way, weren't you? Killed 'erself, didn't she?'

'I offered to marry 'er, as God is my witness,' Harold blustered. 'I even bought 'er a ring.'

'She must 'ave realized that life with you was goin' to be a bloomin' misery. I'm not sayin' as 'ow she was right to tek 'er own life but she was a good girl 'fore you got your 'ands on 'er.'

'I've tried to mek amends for my earlier misdeeds,' said Harold. 'I've served God as best I know 'ow.'

'Aye,' said Ena. 'Bein' a tyrant and feedin' that poor wife of yours so as she's the size of an 'ouse. Are you plannin' to kill 'er off like you did poor Lily?'

'You're a wicked woman, Ena Sharples. I love my wife. I look after 'er.'

'Don't talk rubbish, man! If that's your idea of lookin' after someone then you've no more sense than an organ-grinder's monkey. 'Ow you can afford to buy 'er enough food I'll never know. People round 'ere are gettin' thinner, not fatter.'

The look on his face told her the answer.

'You've bin stealin', 'aven't you?'

His silence was answer enough. His face had paled and his thin shoulders sagged. 'Food made 'er 'appy,' he said finally.

'A bit of freedom would 'ave made 'er even 'appier, 'Arold Preston,' snapped Ena, jabbing him in the chest with her finger. 'You've been a wicked, wicked man. You lost three girls, and then poor Margaret comes along, wants to get away from 'er unhappy 'ome and she's bloomin' putty in your 'ands. I suppose you thought by mekkin' 'er fat she'd never be able to leave you like the others did.'

He shrugged miserably. 'What are you goin' to do?' he asked.

Ena knew she had him in her power. 'I'm doin' nowt. It's you that 'as got to do summat.'

'What can I do?'

'You tell your Margaret she's comin' to the Mission for the day. Bring your turkey with you and we'll find a way to cook it. I'll ask no questions about 'ow you got it. By God's good grace you might be forgiven one day, but only if you change your ways.'

Harold's chin sank towards his chest. 'I'll do my best.'

'You'll do more than that, 'Arold Preston. If you backslides I shall 'ear about it and your stealin' will come to light. You'll be behind bars 'fore you know what's 'it you.'

Harold sloped back into No. 6 with his head down and with a lot of thinking to do.

When Ena got back to the Mission the news of her party had spread, and most of Coronation Street and beyond seemed to be clamouring on her doorstep. 'Give me a chance to open the door,' she said. 'You're all welcome.'

She stood at the front of the Mission. 'Just bring what food you've got that doesn't need cookin', like a bit o' cake and some mince pies–'

Some wag from the back shouted, 'And then you can feed the five thousand!'

Ena was not deterred. 'I want some big strong lads to set trestle tables up and get chairs round and us women will supply the food.'

'What about the beer?' asked Len Fairclough.

'There'll be no drinkin'. I 'aven't got a licence to sell beer.'

Ena failed to notice the little murmur that went round. She also failed to notice that Len Fairclough and a lad called Percy Sugden left the mission immediately for the Rovers.

Much to Len's surprise it was Jack Walker who answered the door at the Rovers. 'If you can carry a barrel of beer, lads, you can 'ave it with pleasure. My way of saying thanks for savin' our Billy.'

'Well, thanks, Jack,' said Len, 'and a merry Christmas to you and yours.'

Percy suggested a wheelbarrow, and as the allotment holders had collected their belongings there was no problem in borrowing one from Albert Tatlock.

'We'll 'ave to keep the barrel outside,' said Len. 'If Ena Sharples finds it there'll be 'ell to pay.'

They pushed the wheelbarrow to the Mission and hid the barrel behind the dustbin.

'The women won't want to drink beer, Len,' said Percy. 'And what will we do about glasses?'

Len laughed. 'We'll 'ave to drink it from tea cups and the women will 'ave to bring their own drink.'

By one o'clock the tables were covered in white sheets and women were carrying in baskets of food and laying the tables. Excited children ran around, but no one minded.

Having organized everyone, Ena began playing carols on the harmonium. There was no sign of Mr Swindley, who was to have preached at the Christmas Day service. His sermons were often dull so Ena had never felt happier. She could choose the carols to suit herself. This was her kingdom and she was in charge.

Margaret, with Betty on one arm and Maggie on the other, made slow, nervous progress towards the Glad Tidings Mission Hall. Harold's contribution had been to joint the turkey and start frying the pieces on the open fire. 'I've no idea 'ow long it will take,' he said, as smoke billowed around the room. 'I needs to pray,' he told his wife. 'I'll come along later.'

Betty had been amazed by her father's changed attitude since Ena had spoken to him. He was subdued but he'd patted Margaret's arm and told her to enjoy herself. Betty feared that her mother wouldn't, that people would stare or make fun of her, but when they arrived there was such a jolly atmosphere and Bessie Tatlock said, 'Nice to see you all. Would you ladies like to 'elp with putting the paper serviettes round?' Betty was even more amazed when her mother joined in with the carol singing.

Ida Barlow brought home-made Christmas crackers for the children and some decorations for the table. Bessie had been delighted with her dress and had worn it for the day. When she received compliments from Dot and Sally, and told them Ida had made it, they praised Ida's flair and asked if she could make dresses for them too. Ida was delighted: she was good at something and she couldn't wait to tell Frank.

After a short time Betty and Maggie stopped worrying about their mother. She had to sit on two chairs but Bessie and Minnie took her under their wing and they could see that she was happier than she'd been in years. Sally let her cuddle little Clark. 'Doesn't that look pretty?' she said, holding up the baby so that he could see the table decoration of twigs stuck into a flower pot covered with green crêpe paper, each twig strung with silver milk-bottle tops. 'I just wish your gran could 'ave been 'ere to see it.'

Elsie Tanner, Tyrone, Chalky and Norman arrived after everyone else. Tyrone was the only sober one. Elsie deposited her children near the Hayes sisters, who seemed more than happy to look after everyone's off-spring and were showing the older children how to make crêpe-paper hats. Out of the corner of her eye, Elsie saw Len signalling her and Dot towards the back door. Dot preferred to stay with the lads. 'You go, Elsie,' she said, giving her a little push. 'He probably wants a kiss under the mistletoe.'

'Fat chance,' said Elsie, laughing.

Outside, Elsie stared at the beer barrel in amazement. 'Who the 'eck gave you that?'

'Jack Walker's 'ome on leave. 'E did.'

'I've brought me own booze,' said Elsie. 'And I'm goin' to slip some vodka into Ena Sharples's squash. We'll be doin' the conga and the 'okey-cokey before she knows what's 'it 'er.' Then she laughed. 'If we sing "Roll Out The Barrel" don't, for Gawd's sake, do owt daft, will you?'

Len smiled. 'Elsie?'

'What?'

'Give us a kiss.'

Elsie pushed him away, laughing. 'You find some mistletoe and I might just oblige, but only one. I 'aven't kissed any of my boys yet.'

Len turned away to refill his cup from the beer barrel. He didn't want Elsie to see how disappointed he was.

Two turkeys cooked in pieces arrived burnt, the Brussels sprouts turned to mush, the potatoes were as hard as iron but no one cared. Only the arrival of a policeman with the man in the black coat caused a hush.

Ena left her harmonium, wondering why she felt a little unsteady.

'Mrs Ena Sharples?' queried the policeman.

'What's 'e doin' here?'

'His name is Ruben Holliman and he's Dieter Holliman's uncle.'

Ena stared at the tall gaunt man. Now that she looked at him closely there was a slight resemblance. 'The lad doesn't seem to know owt about you,' she said suspiciously.

'He doesn't remember me,' said Ruben Holliman. 'But let me explain. I've changed. The war has changed me. I begged my brother to get out of Germany in 1938 but he was a doctor and he wanted to stay. He encouraged his wife Irana and Dieter to leave for England before war broke out.'

'Why didn't you speak up before, man?' asked Ena. 'You've got a tongue in your 'ead.'

'I tried, Mrs Sharples, but when I saw how well and happy Dieter seemed, I thought it best to let him stay where he was. I believe a Mrs Minnie Caldwell is looking after him?'

'Aye, and she loves 'im like 'er own, so you tread carefully with 'er.'

'I am so very grateful, Mrs Sharples,' he said. 'Dieter is the only family I've managed to trace. My brother and sister are somewhere in Poland in one of the camps.'

'I'll be off, then' said the policeman, 'as it's all sorted now.'

'On no you don't, lad,' said Ena sternly. 'You stay awhile and 'elp yourself to whatever you want.'

'A few minutes then, missus,' he said, taking off his helmet.

'As for you, Mr Holliman, don't stand around like a stick of rhubarb, go and mek yourself known to that nephew of yours. And don't go upsettin' Minnie Caldwell.'

Elsie Tanner and her friends made sure Ena played all their favourites. They danced the conga along Coronation Street and Tyrone even persuaded Ena to do the hokey-cokey with him and managed to kiss her on both cheeks. She'd supped enough vodka-laced squash to enjoy it. 'It's the best Christmas

292

I've ever 'ad,' she said.

Elsie, in her own haze of alcohol, looked around the Glad Tidings Mission Hall with its balloons, paper-chains, laughing children, and even Martha Longhurst joining in, and thought most people would say it was their best Christmas ever. Except, of course, that so many loved ones were not there to share it.

'To absent friends,' said Albert Tatlock, raising his cup of beer.

'To absent friends,' everyone chorused.

CHAPTER NINETEEN

Winter 1945: Dresden Destroyed by Allied Air Power. City Burns for Seven Days and Eight Nights

Annie Walker knew she would never forget Christmas 1944. Jack's leave had been a disaster. And, in Annie's opinion, it was all due to Ena Sharples.

On Christmas Day Jack had paid John Barnstable a visit. He never told her what was said, and she didn't ask, but Jack was as cold as ice and John hadn't contacted her since. Jack had also taken an instant dislike to Teresa. 'I reckon,' he'd said, 'that she was the cause. If she 'adn't been around to look after the kids you wouldn't 'ave been able to get up to owt.' Annie vehemently denied any wrongdoing but Jack refused to listen or speak to her. She saw a side of him that she'd never seen before and she supposed the war had hardened him.

As he left, two days after Christmas, he'd said, 'The war will end soon, Annie, and when I get back I want you to get rid of Teresa. I want things to be as they were. If you get up to owt I shall 'ear about it and, believe me, there'll be real trouble.'

Annie nodded wordlessly. Jack was never one to rant and rave or even raise his voice, but she found his cold, deliberate tone far more frightening. He'd always had a stubborn streak and while before the war she had always been able to get her own way, now she realized it wouldn't be so easy. Her dreams of living in the country with either man were shattered. And it was all due to the interference of Ena Sharples. Jack had mentioned a letter but hadn't said who'd sent it, but there was only one person it could have been. It had taken her weeks of resentful thinking but she'd decided that an eye for an eye was a Biblical reference that Ena would understand.

Ena's job and her home at the Glad Tidings Mission Hall were, of course, dependent on her good behaviour. Providing alcohol on the premises was strictly forbidden and Annie reasoned that if she told the Mission authorities someone had stolen a barrel of beer and Ena had appeared to be drunk then it would be goodbye Ena. The small fact that Jack had given Len Fairclough the beer, Annie reasoned, wasn't important. Jack wasn't around to put his side of the story and who would believe Len Fairclough?

It had taken weeks for Annie to decide on this course of action but the fact that she hadn't heard from either John or Jack since his leave had fuelled her desire for vengeance. She'd sent the letter three days before. So now was the time to tell Ena. Annie was going to have the pleasure of her revenge – tonight.

After Elsie Tanner's paying guests had returned to their units Elsie was left hoping that others would turn up, but no one did. Sally and Dot seemed content to stay at home more now, especially since fog, sleet and snow made going out at night such an effort. The winter and the war wore on, queues got longer, rations were cut and coal was in short supply. Elsie was now on short time at Elliston's and the munitions factories no longer offered overtime. Most people had no spare money and few GIs were to be seen these days.

Elsie had seen a bit more of Len Fairclough but they usually landed up arguing, mostly about trivial things. This time it was her curtain rail: Len kept saying it needed doing but she quite enjoyed irritating the ARP wardens. 'Oh all right, Len,' she agreed eventually. 'Just stop mitherin' me. You can do it tomorrow.'

'Best if I do it tonight,' he said. She was about to argue when the ARP wardens knocked on her door and when she didn't reply, yelled through the letterbox. Elsie was outraged and had yelled back. 'Don't you know the bloody war is near over? You're power mad, you lot.'

'I told you,' said Len. 'I'll do it now before you get fined. Me leg's improvin' all the time, if that's what's botherin' you.'

'We 'aven't 'ad a bombin' raid since Christmas,' said Elsie, 'but if it meks yer 'appy yer can fix it and I'll mek yer a corned-beef sandwich for yer trouble.'

'It's no trouble,' said Len. 'I like doin' things for you.'

Elsie noticed the look in his eye. 'Give over, Len, or I'll change me mind.'

After he'd fixed the rail they sat drinking tea, smoking and chatting. 'What are you goin' to do after the war, Elsie?'

Elsie shrugged. 'I don't think that far ahead.'

'Well, you ought to – the war will end this

year. What will you do if Arnold comes marchin' 'ome?'

Elsie laughed. 'I'll 'it 'im over the 'ead with a frying-pan.'

'What about your Eyetie friend?'

Elsie tensed. 'What about 'im? I do wish you'd call 'im by his name. Anyway, I 'aven't 'eard from 'im since before Christmas and I haven't seen 'im in months.'

Len stubbed out his cigarette in the brass ashtray and said cautiously, 'Elsie, 'as it ever crossed your mind 'e might be married?'

Contrary to Len's expectations, Elsie wasn't riled. 'I know a married man from five paces. 'E 'ad nicely darned socks but 'e said 'is mother did 'is mendin'. Anyway, 'e 'ad too much money to be married.'

'What if 'e comes marchin' 'ome and wants you to divorce Arnold and marry 'im?'

'I dunno. I know I'd do a lot for 'im but I wouldn't darn 'is socks.'

'A man wouldn't marry you for bein' owt like an 'ousewife.'

Elsie stared at Len. 'Is that supposed to be a ruddy compliment?'

'Tek it 'ow you please. I just wish you'd tread carefully.'

Elsie began to get irritated. He was always

warning her about something. 'Look 'ere, Len. I'm not sixteen any more. I've seen a bit o' life–'

'No, you 'aven't, Elsie,' he interrupted. 'All you've done is seen a lot of men and made a bit of cash out of it.'

'You've got a bloody cheek,' she exploded. 'What gives you the right? You come 'ere pretendin' you're me best mate when all you really want is me body same as other blokes.'

Len jumped up from his chair. 'That isn't true, you stupid woman,' he shouted. 'I want to *marry* yer not bloody *buy* yer.'

'Well, I wouldn't marry you, Len Fair-clough, if you was the only man without a wooden leg in the whole ruddy world.'

Len made for the door, then turned. He was calmer now. 'I'll tell you this, Elsie, love. You and me was meant to be together and all your life you'll 'ave regrets because you'll never find another man who'll think as much of you as I do.'

'Wanna bet on that one, Len?' she said defiantly.

He didn't answer. He knew he was right. Where Elsie Tanner was concerned he was always right.

Betty Preston walked to work in the rain. She hadn't heard from Ted for a while but things at home had improved. Her mother was losing weight, she went out for short walks and she had started doing a bit of housework and shopping. But just as Margaret seemed to be blooming, Harold was fading. He still read his Bible but he was much quieter and he seemed to get thinner and greyer. All in all, though, Betty was happy. She was convinced that Ted would come back for her soon. He'd promised he would.

When she arrived at Earnshaw's to clock in there was a message for her. The supervisor wanted to see her. Hilda Ogden had had the same message and they stood side by side waiting for the supervisor to appear.

Once the klaxon had sounded they could hear the sound of heavy metal clanging and the factory coming alive. Betty grew restless and Hilda, whose swelling stomach never looked the same two days running, patted her bump. After a while Betty asked, "Ow's your Stanley?'

'Champion,' said Hilda. "E's a prisoner-of-war in Italy.'

'I'm sorry to 'ear that.'

'Don't be,' said Hilda. "E says 'e's quite 'appy and it's better than bein' in the glasshouse.'

'Is 'e pleased about the baby?'

Hilda smiled. "E's real 'appy. I'm ever so proud of 'im. When 'e was in the glasshouse they said 'e was a model prisoner so I know 'e'll keep out of trouble in Italy. 'E says 'e 'ates the food there but 'e's always bin fussy. 'E says I should move in with his mam, but I dunno – I don't think she likes me much. She thinks I talk a lot.'

'Aye,' said Betty, trying to keep a straight face. 'I wonder why.'

The supervisor turned up then, looking grim. 'I expect you know why I want to see you.'

'No, I don't,' said Hilda. 'I've done nowt wrong.'

'I'm sorry, but we 'ave to lay the two of you off. Last in, first out, I'm afraid that's the policy.'

Both Betty and Hilda stood there in a state of shock. The supervisor looked at Hilda and said gently, 'In your condition, 'Ilda, you wouldn't 'ave bin able to carry on much longer anyway.'

Hilda, determined not to cry, wasn't going to leave without some sort of protest.

'You could 'ave kept us on till the end of the war.'

'The war's nearly over, 'Ilda,' she said. 'They won't need munitions any more.'

'They could mek something else,' said Hilda. 'Just cast-offs, that's all we are.'

'I'm sorry, there's nothing I can do. It's a fact of war.'

Betty slipped her coat back on. It was a blow but she realized it wasn't anybody's fault. 'Come on, 'Ilda, let's go 'ome,' she suggested.

Hilda wasn't prepared to go without having her say. 'Us women 'ave kept this war bloomin' going. It ain't right.'

'I can't stand 'ere all day, arguing,' said the supervisor, taking envelopes from her pocket. 'The bosses want you to go today, so I've got you a week's pay and a week extra. I couldn't do better than that for you.'

Hilda snatched her envelope. 'Well, thanks for nothing. You can 'ave this while you're at it.' Hilda reached a hand inside her skirt, pulled out a cushion and threw it on the floor. 'And I'm reet glad to be rid of that and yer rotten job.' She flounced to the door.

Betty and the supervisor stood, eyes fixed on the cushion on the floor. They couldn't have been more surprised if a baby itself had been lying there.

Two grim-faced senior members of the Mission Hall's board of governors arrived at Ena's flat at just after ten a.m. They came straight to the point. 'We've come about the serious business of you supplying alcohol on Christmas Day,' said Archie Barnes. Ena had known Archie for years: he was an assistant bank manager, unmarried, nearing fifty with sparse hair and a sparse body that needed large braces to hold his trousers up.

'I never did,' protested Ena. 'You know I'm a stickler for the rules, Mr Barnes. Christmas Day we only 'ad tea and lemonade and orange squash.'

'That's as maybe, Mrs Sharples,' said Cecil Adcocks, a bachelor nearing retirement, who Ena thought had a face as bland as a dumpling and a personality to match. 'We've had a report, you see, concerning a stolen barrel of beer and much drunkenness.'

'As God is my witness,' said Ena, 'I don't know what you're talkin' about. I saw nobody who was drunk and I would 'ave noticed. There isn't much that gets past me.'

'We do know you're diligent, Mrs

Sharples,' said Adcocks, 'but the fact remains that this is what we've heard.'

'Well, you've 'eard wrong, Mr Adcocks. And I'd like to know where you 'eard this malicious gossip.'

'We can't divulge that, Mrs Sharples.'

Ena stared at both men. She would have liked to rant and rave at them, but her job and home depended on their relying on her to run the Mission properly.

'I can mek a good guess as to who 'as told you this pack of lies,' she said. 'It's someone who's 'oldin' a grudge against me. If you leave it wi' me I'm sure the culprit will admit they've been doin' nowt but mekkin' mischief.'

Both Adcocks and Barnes looked undecided. 'Will you excuse us a minute, Mrs Sharples?' said Archie Barnes. 'We need to talk this through.'

Ena stood outside the vestry door trying to eavesdrop, but she could hear nothing until they raised their voices slightly and even then she couldn't make out any individual words. It seemed ages before they reappeared, unsmiling. 'We've decided,' said Archie Barnes, 'after a lot of heart-searching, to allow you three days to write us an account of the events of Christmas Day. If, as you say, this is merely malicious gossip then maybe the person in question would be willing to retract the allegations.' He paused to cough nervously. 'There's nothing we can do to save your job, Mrs Sharples, if you can't satisfy us that you were unaware of the situation. And we shall inform the police about the stealing of a barrel of beer from licensed premises.'

Ena swallowed and took a deep breath. 'You'll 'ave it down in writing and I can promise you that the owner of the evil tongue will repent 'er ways. I'm one that believes God is on the side of the righteous and I'm a God-fearin' woman.'

'You have three days, Mrs Sharples, to prove that,' said Cecil. 'Let's hope you're right.'

When they'd gone Ena could hardly contain her temper. She'd sort Annie Walker out if it was the last thing she ever did – she'd sort the snooty bitch out if she had to face tanks or fire-throwers or even a barrage of V2s. 'I'll deal with her,' she said aloud. Then she got down on her knees to ask the Lord God for guidance on retribution. She only spoke to Jesus when she was in a good mood. The God of the Old Testament was the one she needed now.

Elsie Tanner sat with her feet in a bowl of mustard water and her eyes and nose streaming. Both Dennis and Linda had got whooping-cough and none of them was getting any sleep. Now Elsie was trying to cure her cold. She'd taken aspirin and hot toddies but she didn't feel any better. The day before she'd squashed both children into the pram and taken them to the gasworks again to let them breathe in the fumes. She'd tried it three times – it was supposed to cure the whooping-cough but it hadn't worked so far and most of the time they lay weak and listless on her bed.

She was drying her feet when she heard the back door open. 'We've got the plague 'ere so you've been warned.'

''Ello, Elsie.'

In her shock at the sound of Arnold's rough voice she jumped and knocked the mustard water over the rug. She ignored the pool of water, pulled her dressing-gown around her and tried to keep her voice level. 'What are you doin' 'ere, Arnold? I thought you said you was never coming back.'

'I've bin wounded. Some shrapnel in me chest. Where else would I go to but me own 'ome?'

'I don't want any trouble, Arnold.'

Even as she spoke Elsie could see he didn't look capable of trouble. He'd lost weight, his face was grey and his eyes sunken. 'I'm dog tired, Elsie,' he said. 'Will you mek me a brew and then I'll get me 'ead down.'

Elsie felt unnerved by such a subdued Arnold. She made him tea and used the last of her butter to make him a potted-meat sandwich. 'I 'ear you've bin enjoyin' yourself,' he said, as he sipped his tea.

'You've 'eard wrong, then, Arnold. I've 'ad payin' guests, that's all.'

'More bed than breakfast, I bet,' he said smiling. 'You always were a lousy cook.'

Elsie stared at him. At fifteen she'd thought him tall and handsome. Now she saw a sad, broken man and she felt herself warming towards him. She'd never love him like she loved Steve but Arnold was still her husband and she should try to make the best of it.

'Lovely sandwiches, pet,' he said. 'I'll get meself off to bed now. 'Ow are the kids?'

'They've 'ad the whooping-cough – they're still asleep.'

'I won't wake them, then,' he said.

After an hour Elsie went upstairs and

peeped in on Arnold. He'd folded his uniform neatly and hung it up. He lay on his back, his hair and face clammy-looking. At that moment he reminded her of Dennis when he was poorly. He seemed to be a changed man, and Elsie felt a real wave of optimism that once the war was over Arnold might prove a good husband – if that was what she wanted.

Arnold stayed for nearly two weeks. He gained weight and the colour came back to his cheeks. He played with Dennis and Linda, and only went to the pub three times on his own. Even though he got a bit nasty he didn't threaten her, and Elsie's optimism grew.

On the day he left to go back to sea Elsie offered to go with him to the station. He shook his head. 'You stay put, Elsie, love,' he said, kissing her. 'I want to remember you waving me off from the front doorstep.'

With Dennis and Linda in her arms, she waved until Arnold was out of sight.

Elsie felt near to tears. She had enjoyed having him home and so had the kids. It was only later when she went to the teapot where she kept her savings that she found he'd taken half the money. 'You sod!' she said aloud. But later, when she'd calmed down, she realized he could have taken *all* the money. Her Arnold did have a conscience, after all. And he was her husband, she told herself, so he was entitled to half.

CHAPTER TWENTY

Spring 1945: Hitler and Eva Braun Commit Suicide. Tuesday 8 May VE-Day. Victory in Europe.

Ena Sharples had walked with head held high and shoulders back towards the Rovers for her showdown with Annie Walker. In her own private war she'd been determined that, like Germany, she would have Annie Walker signing a peace declaration. But Annie's signature would be immediate.

She'd seen Annie's wary glance as she entered the Rovers and she ordered a half of mild and said nothing. She's just stared. It was when she was ordering her second half that Annie had asked, 'Is anything wrong, Mrs Sharples?'

Ena waited until her beer was poured before saying through gritted teeth, 'Nowt that an announcement to all your customers wouldn't solve.'

'What are you talking about, Mrs Sharples?'

Ena ignored her question. Annie Walker knew full well what it was about. 'Mind you,' said Ena, in a loud voice, 'after I've said my piece to everyone 'ere I doubt you'll 'ave any more customers.'

Annie looked flustered, much to Ena's delight. 'I think,' said Annie, 'it might be better if we talk in private.'

Ena looked at her milk stout. 'I'll drink this first,' she said. 'It'll give you time to have a serious think about the sin you've committed.'

Annie raised her eyebrows but said nothing. There were far too many people around and they were beginning to take an interest.

Ena rejoined Minnie and Martha in the Snug. 'What did she say, Ena?'

'I 'aven't said owt yet, just that she should think on 'er sins. I reckon she's as rattled as Lord Haw-Haw.'

'Do be careful, Ena,' said Minnie. 'You don't want to mek things worse.'

'Worse? Don't be so daft, Minnie Caldwell. 'Ow could things be worse? I'll lose me job and me 'ome if I can't get Annie Walker to tell the truth.'

'There *was* beer being drunk,' said Martha, 'and you did look as if you'd 'ad a drink or two.'

'Who asked you, Martha Longhurst?'

Martha sniffed. 'I'm entitled to me opinions.'

'Not while I'm 'ere suppin' ale you're not,' said Ena, glancing over to where Annie was trying to serve several people at once. 'If you've got nowt useful to say don't bother to open your trap.'

'There's no need to get nasty with us, Ena,' said Minnie. 'We're only tryin' to 'elp you.'

'I don't need 'elp. And your 'elp is as much use as a penn'orth of soap to wash an elephant.'

Both Minnie and Martha fell silent. Talking to Ena in the mood she was in was a waste of their breath.

Once Ena had finished her drink she stood up and walked over to Albert Tatlock. 'Albert, I've got to 'ave words with Annie Walker. Tek over the bar, will you?'

Albert nodded. 'Aye. You're not up to owt, are you, Ena?'

Ena shook her head. 'Nowt that that woman 'asn't brought on 'erself.'

In Annie Walker's parlour the two women faced each other sitting at either end of the dining-table with a lace runner and a spider plant between them.

'So, Annie Walker,' said Ena slowly, 'your plan is to mek me lose me job and me 'ome by tellin' downright lies to me gaffers.'

'You had beer on the premises,' said Annie. 'And I heard you were drunk.'

'I was 'eck as like. I drank orange squash all day. You're just doin' it out o' spite because I wrote to your Jack.'

'Are you surprised, Mrs Sharples? After all, you tried to break up my marriage.'

Ena was indignant. 'I did no such thing. For a woman who thinks she's well above 'er station in life you can be as dim as Minnie Caldwell. I was tryin' to keep a family together. Do you think any stepfather is goin' to think as much of your kiddies as their own flesh and blood?'

Annie didn't answer so Ena repeated herself. 'Flesh and blood and the sacred oath you made Jack, that's what matters.'

Annie's lower lip dropped slightly and Ena could see that she was fiddling with her wedding ring.

'Now, I've 'eard as 'ow I was tricked about the beer,' continued Ena, 'but I didn't *know* they 'ad it outside and that meks me an innocent party.'

'Well, you *should* have known,' snapped

313

Annie. 'The Mission was your responsibility.'

'We all mek mistakes, Annie Walker, but your main mistake was in sayin' Len Fairclough stole that barrel of beer. He could've gone to prison but 'e went to see Adcocks and Barnes and they agreed not to tek any further action until Jack 'imself could be contacted.'

'Oh, my God,' murmured Annie.

'You might well call on God, Annie Walker. When your Jack comes 'ome for good I reckon there's some questions 'e'll want to ask you 'imself. And I know Jack. 'E might be a gentleman but 'e's got some passion in 'is soul and knowin' what war does to people, 'e'll be a different man from the one you remember.'

Annie stared ahead, then at the floor. Ena Sharples was an old witch but she was right. Jack had already changed. She had no choice. 'What do you want me to do?'

'You can send a letter explainin' you told a lie and as 'ow you've lived to regret it. You can also say I knew nothin' about the beer.'

There was only a short pause before Annie muttered, 'Very well, Mrs Sharples.'

As Ena left she fired a parting shot. 'You think you're better than any of us, Annie

Walker, but you're a woman who 'as morals to suit 'erself and one who doesn't know when she's well off.' Ena paused and opened the door into the pub and said loudly so that everyone could hear, 'You're worse than that trollop Elsie Tanner – only at least she don't pretend to 'ave any morals. She might sell 'er body but you'd sell your ruddy soul.'

Having had her two halves and a pound of flesh, Ena signalled to Minnie and Martha that it was time to leave. They walked out together, Ena with her head held high. She would have felt as proud as any prize-fighter, except that she'd scored a knockout in the first round and victory had come too soon for her to really relish the moment.

Ida Barlow and Bessie Tatlock heard the news of Hitler's death on the wireless on 1 May. Bessie came straight round in case Ida hadn't heard it.

'At long last he's done for himself,' said Bessie.

'About time too,' agreed Ida, putting on the kettle for a celebratory cuppa. 'It *is* nearly over *now*, isn't it?'

'Course it is, love. Albert says only a few more days. Mind you, there's still the Japs to worry about.'

'I've got used to the war,' murmured Ida. 'It's like it's never been any different.'

Bessie smiled. 'One day we might look back on these years and say they were the best years ever.'

Ida didn't believe that, but she'd managed without Frank, and, thanks to Bessie, she'd found a new talent. When the children were older, she decided, she'd look for a job outside. She hadn't really known the meaning of ambition before but now she had visions of her own little dress hop. It was a dream that kept her going. She was sure Frank would be delighted that she could now help out with the housekeeping money. She'd got a little bit put by and she'd treat Frank to the best meal he'd ever had. She just knew that as soon as the war was over the shops would be bulging with meat and cheese and butter.

'It'll be grand, won't it, Bessie?'

'Let's 'ope so, love.'

Since Arnold's visit Elsie had been in the doldrums. Money was tight now. Dot and Sally had rallied round, bringing scones and vegetable pies to cheer her up, but there had been no more paying guests. One blessing was that Elliston's short time had ended when they landed a large contract for demob suits so at least Elsie had full wages. Another blessing was that Dennis and Linda had fully recovered from whooping-cough.

On evenings when she didn't go out and the kids were asleep and the house was quiet, Elsie sat smoking and wondering what the end of the war would bring. She tried to pin her future hopes on Arnold, but Steve Tanner was often in her thoughts and dreams. She still longed to see him one more time, but deep down she doubted she would. What man in his right mind would want a woman with two young children in tow and no money? Steve would have to rebuild his life, but she couldn't believe he'd manage that with the three of them. Anyway, for all she knew he was a prisoner-of-war in Europe or, worse, fighting the Japanese.

As for Antonio, she'd heard nothing from him. Like a few other men in her life, he had become a fond memory. Just have to keep hoping for something better, she told herself. She was sure of one thing: one day her prince would come.

Betty Preston wasn't used to idleness.

Margaret had resumed most of the house-work and the cooking, which left Betty either standing in queues at the shops or at the labour exchange. Now that the war was almost at an end, Betty's hopes of Ted writing diminished. She had another admirer, though – a lad from Weatherfield who had been conscripted to work in the mines. He lived in Rosamund Street with his gran, his name was Joe Pattishall, he was twenty-four and she'd been to the pictures with him twice. He was quiet and shy, and when Betty had said no to being kissed he hadn't minded.

'I can wait,' he said. 'Me gran says a good girl is worth waitin' for.'

As Betty stood in her second queue of the day at the labour exchange, listening to an elderly lady with a voice like a foghorn shouting 'Next!', she realised what was wrong with Joe: his opinions were all his gran's. He had none of his own and if Betty didn't agree with his dear old gran then he got sulky and defensive. He takes me to the pictures, thought Betty. I don't have to marry him. Although Betty would have liked children, she'd seen too much of her mother's marriage to risk marrying the wrong person.

'Next!' came the shout. 'Next!' the woman repeated.

Betty, startled, moved to the counter. 'Here's one might suit you, Miss Preston – usherette at the Bijou.'

'That'll suit me grand,' said Betty. Now she wouldn't need Joe or his gran's opinions ever again. She smiled sweetly at the woman with the foghorn voice and was given details of the hours and the pay. If she went to see the manager she could start whenever she liked. The money was poor but it was a job, and she'd get to see all the latest films.

On her way home she caught a glimpse of her father, black tailcoat waving in the breeze and the sun glinting on his ivory-handled walking stick. He seemed to be moving more slowly than usual so she easily caught up with him. 'I've got a job, Dad,' she said cheerfully.

He stopped and took a deep breath. 'What doing?'

'Usherette at the Bijou.'

He didn't answer but carried on walking. They had just turned into Tile Street when he stopped. Betty had noticed how pale he'd grown of late but now he seemed ashen and grey and his upper lip was beaded with sweat.

'Are you all right, Dad?' she asked anxiously.

He struggled to answer her and when he did it was in a whisper. 'Fetch your mother.'

Betty ran the few yards to No. 6 and her mother tried to hurry out to Harold – but by the time they reached him he'd collapsed on the pavement. Margaret knelt clumsily beside him and put an ear to his moving lips. Betty stood looking on, hardly able to believe what had happened. Someone called an ambulance, but by the time it arrived Harold Preston was dead.

Betty and her mother walked slowly back to the house. Neither of them cried. Once they were indoors Betty asked, 'What did he say, Mam?'

Margaret gave a wry smile. 'That he was on his way to meet his Maker.'

At the sight of Betty's face Margaret said, 'Don't fret too much, pet. He never did live in this world – he was always half in the next.'

In the days that followed Betty often wondered if learning of her job at the Bijou had killed her father, but then she remembered his slow decline since Ena Sharples had spoken to him at Christmas. Whatever had she said to him?

On her way home from work Elsie marvelled at how Coronation Street had been transformed. Bunting and balloons had been strung up, trestle tables opened in readiness for the day that had finally come – VE-Day. Victory in Europe. Somehow the sight of the decorations waving in the breeze meant more than all the speeches and the long-winded negotiations since Hitler's death. Tomorrow really was the war's end.

Elsie paused at her back door. A parcel wrapped in brown paper had been placed on her back step. Antonio. She picked it up, guessing by its weight that it contained cigarettes, and was just about to go indoors when she heard a creak. She turned to see Antonio appear from the privy.

'Elsie, my lovely,' he said, as he swept her into his arms and carried her indoors.

Although she was pleased to see him she wasn't going to be swayed by his romantic gesture. 'Why 'ave I 'eard nowt from you before now?' she asked.

'It's been difficult. But I've thought about you every day.'

She noticed now that he was unshaven and the civvies he wore were creased and looked as if he had worn them for some time. 'What's up?' she asked.

'I need a drink.'

She gave him a whisky, and he drank it neat in one go. 'Are you goin' to tell me what's wrong?' she said, offering him a Woodbine.

He took a deep drag. 'They're after me, Elsie.'

'Who are?'

'The police, the family. Quite a few people.'

'What for? What 'ave you done?'

'I've been a naughty boy. Will you help me get away?'

'Have you killed anyone?'

'No, Elsie. On my mother's life I haven't killed anyone.'

'Tell me what you've done then.'

He stood up and stroked her face. 'I will, my lovely, in time, but now all I want is to hold you in my arms and sleep beside you.'

Elsie thought, but only for a moment. Already he was kissing her and she wanted him. 'You'll need a shave first,' she said. 'I'll be blowed if I'll sleep with a man whose face is as rough as a sow's arse.'

Antonio laughed. 'Elsie, my darling, I've missed you.'

The morning of VE-Day Elsie woke to

find Antonio up and dressed. 'What's the rush?' she asked, still only half awake.

'Do you have any money?'

'About a quid, that's all,' she said, still half asleep.

'What 'appened to all the money I sent you?'

Elsie raised herself up on one arm. 'I didn't realize I was meant to be savin' it for you.'

'I just hoped you'd got some left,' said Antonio, as he sat beside her on the bed and stroked her arm.

'I would 'ave,' she said 'but my 'usband came back and nicked it.'

'Arnold's a devious sod,' he said.

Elsie sat bolt upright. 'You know 'im? You never told me.'

'How do you think I came knockin' at your door? I got your note but you could 'ave been an old bat. Arnold told me you were a looker.'

'Where did you meet 'im?' she asked suspiciously. 'He's in the Navy and you're in the Air Force.'

'In the Naafi.'

'Oh,' said Elsie. She had other questions to ask him but Dennis wandered into the bedroom, saying that Linda was wet, so

Elsie knew her day had begun in earnest. 'It's a street party today, pet. War's over.'

Dennis grinned happily and yanked at his falling pyjama trousers but he was far too young to know what a street party was and the war was all he'd ever known.

Minnie Caldwell wet-combed Dieter's hair and pulled his jumper down. 'You 'ave scrubbed up well, pet. You'll 'ave a lovely time today.'

'Will there be cakes and ice-cream?' he asked.

'There'll be cakes. Everybody's making summat. Don't know about ice-cream, though.'

If Minnie was honest she didn't want the war to end. Dieter's uncle Ruben was planning to make a home for his nephew, possibly in Weatherfield so that Dieter could stay at Bessie Street School. Since Christmas he had visited several times and Minnie realized that soon it would just be her, Mabel and her mother, who now slept both day and night. Dieter had brightened Minnie's life and she prayed every night that he wouldn't forget her.

'Time to go, lad,' said Minnie. He slipped his small hand into hers and Minnie fought back her tears. Plenty of time for that when 'e's gone, she told herself. 'Let's go and listen to what Mr Churchill 'as to say.'

'Will he be in our street, Auntie?'

Minnie smiled. 'Only 'is voice. It's coming over the loudspeaker at three o'clock.'

Elsie had rushed around all morning. Finally Linda and Dennis looked presentable and they ran round excitedly, knowing that something different was going to happen.

'Aren't you coming out?' she asked Antonio.

He shook his head. 'I've got to lay low.' He patted the children's heads. 'If something should 'appen, Elsie, sweetheart, remember you're my one and only and I'll be back.'

Elsie blew him a kiss. How many women had heard that routine? Antonio wasn't the man she had thought he was. He seemed smaller, shabbier and poorer, somehow less foreign and exotic. But last night he had said he loved her. And that meant a lot to Elsie.

Today Coronation Street lived up to its name, thought Elsie, all brightened up for a real celebration, with tables laid with cakes and trifles and sausage rolls and sandwiches, bunting, balloons and Union Flags, and excited children screaming and laughing. The adults, including servicemen, stood around silently waiting for Winston Churchill to speak. They all knew it was a moment they'd never forget.

It was at about ten to three that Elsie saw the police car stop at the top of the road. They had come for Antonio, she was sure of that. With any luck they'd wait till the speech was over. She grabbed Len Fairclough by the arm. 'Len, you've got to 'elp me. Get a few lads in uniform into my 'ouse. I want them to 'old up the police for a while.'

'Who is it you're 'idin?'

'Antonio.'

'I might 'ave known. You're a bloody fool, Elsie.'

'Don't argue, Len. I've got to warn him.'

'He'll get caught. If not by the civilian police, the MPs will get 'im.'

Elsie dashed through the crowd and into No. 11. 'Antonio, you've got to get out – police are 'ere.'

Antonio grabbed his small suitcase and began throwing in the few clothes he'd brought. Then he started to kiss her. 'There's no time for that,' she said, pushing him towards the back door. 'Just get going.'

As he opened the door two burly police-men rushed in. Within seconds he was handcuffed. 'What's 'e done?' asked Elsie, hanging on to the policeman's sleeve. ''E's a flyin' instructor.' The policeman smiled grimly. 'Is that what 'e told you, love? Truth is 'e worked as a Naafi supervisor and robbed it blind in the process.'

Elsie couldn't resist it. She gave Antonio a stinging slap across the face. 'I love you, Elsie,' was all he said and he was still shouting, 'I love you,' as they dragged him away.

Elsie wondered how she could have been so easily deceived. Then she took a deep breath and resolved to go out into the Street with her head held high.

Len was nowhere to be seen, and Antonio was being bundled into the police car and all eyes were on her.

'Len Fairclough, I want to speak to you,' she yelled into the crowd.

But the crackly sound of the loudspeaker stopped everyone in their tracks. Even the children were quiet to hear Winston Churchill's speech. His resonant tone reached all of the crowd in Coronation Street. The war with Germany was officially over, he told them, and a great cheer went up as he finished. Ena Sharples began singing 'Rule, Britannia' at the top of her voice. Everyone joined in, and even Elsie forgot Antonio's abrupt departure as two soldiers linked arms with her.

Later, as darkness fell, a bonfire was lit on the Red Rec. They burnt effigies of Hitler and sang everything from 'Roll Out The Barrel' to 'It's A Long Way to Tipperary'. Everyone danced, and Elsie Tanner collected several soldiers and kissed them all. She'd eventually found Len with Dot and Sally so she didn't say much except, 'You wait till tomorrow, Len Fairclough, I want words with you.'

He'd had a few drinks and he'd grinned at her. 'Elsie, love, I'm tremblin' in me boots.'

Ida Barlow stood next to Bessie and Albert Tatlock, thinking about Frank. Ena, Martha and Minnie came to join them. 'The men will be 'ome soon, won't they?' Ida said, to no one in particular.

'Don't 'old your breath,' said Ena. 'It'll tek time.'

'It'll be grand when they come,' murmured Ida.

'Aye,' said Ena. 'Things will change.'

Minnie looked towards the lights of

Weatherfield. 'It's champion to see the lights on again.'

They stood, for a moment, enjoying the sight of Weatherfield lit as brightly as a Christmas Tree. 'And did you 'ear Mr Churchill's speech?' Minnie said. 'It fair made me spine tingle. What did 'e say at the end, Ena?'

Ena smiled. 'Trust you not to remember, Minnie Caldwell. 'E said: "Advance Britannia. Long live the cause of freedom. God save the King."'

'Ooh, Ena,' said Minnie. 'Even when you say it, it meks me spine tingle.'

'Don't be so daft, Minnie Caldwell. How about a chorus of "Abide With Me"?'

'Do we 'ave to, Ena?' asked Minnie plaintively.

'Aye. Just because war's over doesn't mean we can forget our Maker.'

Ena began to sing and nobody minded. Slowly everyone joined in, their voices rising up, sombre yet happy.

In a rare moment of silence after the hymn, Ena looked at the happy crowd and gave a thought to those faces that were missing. Some would never return. Others would come back changed. In her eyes, Weatherfield's war was the only one that

counted and Weatherfield had come
through to Victory. Advance, Britannia.
Long live the cause of freedom. God save
the King. Minnie was right. It *did* make her
spine tingle.

The publishers hope that this book has given you enjoyable reading. Large Print Books are especially designed to be as easy to see and hold as possible. If you wish a complete list of our books, please ask at your local library or write directly to:

Magna Large Print Books,
Magna House, Long Preston,
Skipton, North Yorkshire.
BD23 4ND

This Large Print Book, for people
who cannot read normal print,
is published under the auspices of

THE ULVERSCROFT FOUNDATION

Other MAGNA Titles
In Large Print

LYN ANDREWS
Angels Of Mercy

HELEN CANNAM
Spy For Cromwell

EMMA DARCY
The Velvet Tiger

SUE DYSON
Fairfield Rose

J. M. GREGSON
To Kill A Wife

MEG HUTCHINSON
A Promise Given

TIM WILSON
A Singing Grave

RICHARD WOODMAN
The Cruise Of The Commissioner